CLASSIC ROCK CLIMBS
NUMBER 01

D0254196

JOSHUA TREE NATIONAL PARK, CALIFORNIA

by
Randy Vogel

Chockstone Press
Evergreen, Colorado
1997

Classic Rock Climbs: Joshua Tree National Park, California
© 1997 Randy Vogel. All rights reserved. This book or any part thereof may not be reproduced in any form whatsoever, whether by graphic, visual, electronic, or any means other than for brief passages embodied in critical reviews and articles, without the written permission of the publisher.

ISBN: 1-57540-025-1 Classic Rock Climbs series
       1-57540-029-4 Joshua Tree National Park, CA

Published and distributed by
Chockstone Press, Inc.
Post Office Box 3505
Evergreen, CO 80437-3505

PREFACE

Joshua Tree National Park has well over 5,000 climbs, an amount that is daunting to all but the most fanatical local climber. With so many excellent and downright junky routes from which to choose, the visiting or infrequent climber is easily overwhelmed. It is for this latter group that this guide is intended. The nearly 500 routes described represent a variety of some of the best climbs in the Park as well as other adjacent climbs that may be of interest. However, because the Park is so huge, and the classic routes so dispersed, there are literally hundreds of excellent and classic routes that are not included in this guide.

Remember, climbing in our National Parks is a privilege, not an absolute right. Always respect natural environmental values and other users seeking to enjoy the Park. Abuse the privilege and dad can take the car keys away. Yet, in these politically uncertain times, you must do even more. Support legislation, legislators and groups that seek to protect our National Parks and other public lands from the well-financed logging, mining, grazing, development, and privatization interests. Help strengthen, not weaken, laws to protect wildlife, clean air, pure water, and the world our children will inherit. From John Muir to David Brower, climbers have always been at the forefront of the environmental movement. Renew that heritage and your individual commitment, while being vigilant to unfair regulation of climbing disguised as environmental protection.

Several people provided advice, route information, input for this guide, and/or helped check out (i.e., climb) routes. I would like to specifically acknowledge and thank: Alan Bartlett, Kevin Daniels, Bob Gaines, Darrell Hensel, Chris Miller, Todd Swain, and my wife Sarah Tringali. Their assistance, together with those who provided information for previous Josh guides, helped make this book possible.

Randy Vogel

Mike Waugh on Rubicon (5.10c)
Photo: Kevin Powell

TABLE OF CONTENTS

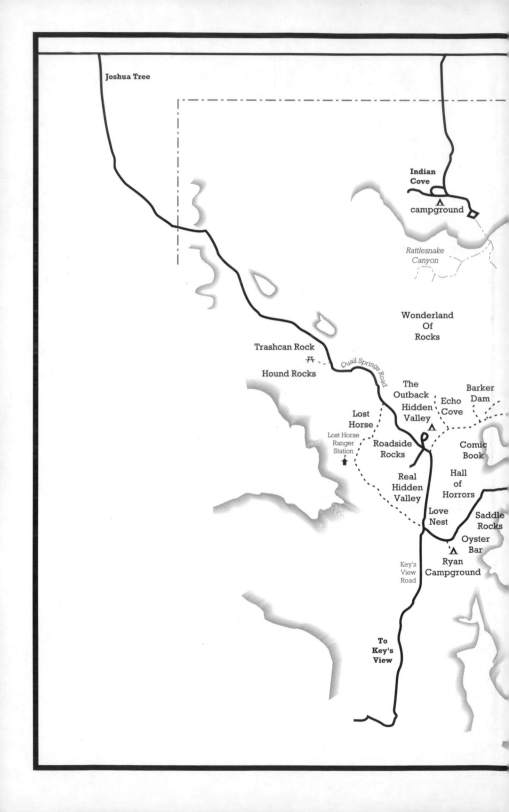

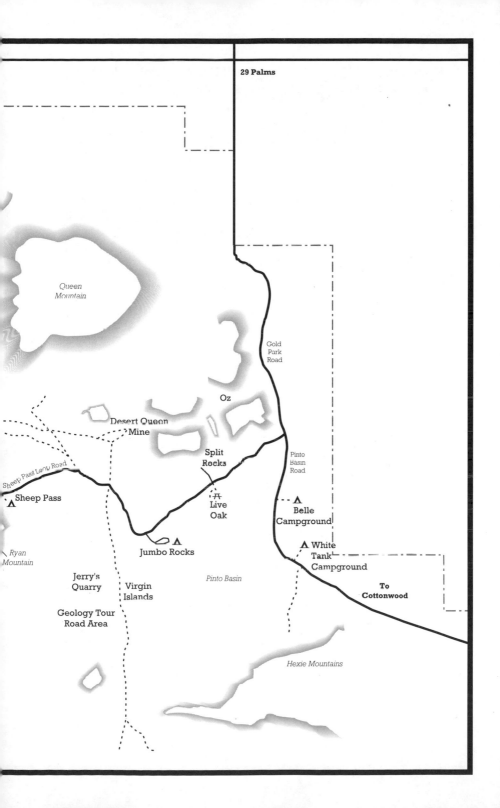

Brandt Allen on Loose Lady (5.10a) Houser Buttress
Photo: Kevin Powell

INTRODUCTION

JOSHUA TREE NATIONAL PARK, CALIFORNIA

Joshua Tree National Park is one of the most popular climbing areas in the world. Climbers from all over the world have enjoyed this truly unique climbing area. This introduction is intended to help you with matters ranging from how to use the book, to how to minimize environmental impacts. There is also information included concerning: how to get to the park, weather, camping, park regulations and, of course, some thoughts on ratings and equipment.

MINIMIZE YOUR IMPACT   Rock climbers constitute a significant percentage of all visitors to this beautiful and often wild part of the Southern California high desert. For this reason climbers must take particular care to insure that their visit to the park has as minimal an impact as possible. Although climbers tend, as a group, to be some of the most environmentally conscientious users, there is a growing, and often irrationally, critical look being taken at climbing activities. It is important that all climbers familiarize themselves with how to use the park in a sound manner. Be responsible. If you witness others engaging in irresponsible behavior, get all over them (in a nice way of course). Unfortunately, in the currently overcharged environment, even the thoughtless act of one individual can affect the rights of everyone. Every climber should support groups that attempt to preserve access and the environment for climbers, such as The Friends of Joshua Tree and The Access Fund.

The Friends of Joshua Tree
PO Box 739
Joshua Tree, CA 92252

The Access Fund
PO Box 17010
Boulder, CO 80308

HOW TO GET TO JOSHUA TREE

Joshua Tree National Park is located in the high desert of eastern Southern California, approximately 140 miles east of Los Angeles and about 35 miles northeast of Palm Springs.

FROM SOUTHERN CALIFORNIA

Los Angeles Area–(plan on 2½ to 3 hours). Take either Interstate 10 or U.S. 60 east to Beaumont/Banning where they merge into Interstate 10.

Orange County Area–(plan on 2 to 2½ hours). Take U.S. 91 east to Riverside, then take U.S. 60 east to Beaumont/Banning where it merges into Interstate 10.

San Diego Area–(plan on 2½ to 3½ hours). Take I-15E (215) north to U.S. 60, then head east to Beaumont/Banning where it merges into Interstate 10.

From Beaumont/Banning continue east on Interstate 10 past the Palm Springs Exit (Highway 111), taking the U.S. 62 Exit north to the town of Joshua Tree. Turn right (south) on Park Blvd. which leads directly to the park's West Entrance some five miles up the road.

FROM THE EAST (THROUGH LAS VEGAS)   Approximately 55 miles west of Las Vegas (on Interstate 15), there is a particularly good shortcut directly toward 29 Palms, via the railroad towns of Cima and Kelso, past the Granite Mountains, crossing Interstate 40, then past Amboy to 29 Palms. However, this road is extremely desolate, and a few miles follow a well-graded dirt road. The alternative (normal) route is to take Interstate 15 to Barstow and take Highway 247 south until it terminates in Yucca Valley. Turn left on Highway 62 to Park Blvd. and into the town of Joshua Tree.

FROM THE BAY AREA AND PACIFIC NORTHWEST   From the San Francisco Bay Area and Pacific Northwest, head south via either Interstate 5 or Highway 99 to Bakersfield. From Bakersfield take Highway 58 east to Barstow (Highway 58 turns into Interstate 40). From Barstow, take Highway 247 south to Lucerne Valley, and continue on Highway 247 to Yucca Valley. Turn left on Highway 62 to Park Blvd. and drive into the town of Joshua Tree.

FROM THE SOUTHWEST   From the southwestern part of the United States (Arizona, New Mexico, etc.), one can take U.S. 10 west until the park can be entered near the City of Indio through the southern (Cottonwood) entrance. Alternatively, one can take Interstate 40 west, then head south to Amboy and eventually to 29 Palms.

ENTRANCE FEES   The National Parks Service imposes an entrance (user) fee. At the time of this writing, the fees were as follows:

$3.00 per walk-in/bicycle rider, bus occupant or motorcycle (good for seven (7) days).

$5.00 per vehicle (no limit on occupants and good for seven days).

$15.00 for the Joshua Tree yearly pass (good for one year from date of purchase, only at Joshua Tree National Park).

$25.00 for the Golden Eagle Pass. The Golden Eagle Pass may be used at all National Parks/Monuments (good for one year, from date of purchase).

CLIMBING SEASON

The best months for climbing are usually late October to early December and March through April. However, there is no such thing as a sure bet with the weather, and some seasons have wonderful Januarys and Februarys and terrible springs. The park receives approximately 7.5 inches of precipitation per year, with nearly 40% falling during the months of July, August and September. Additionally, it is quite possible (but certainly not a sure bet) that temperatures may be quite reasonable even during July, August and September.

CAMPING

Out of the many campgrounds in the park, there are five campgrounds at which climbers will be interested in staying. On many weekends, all of these are congested. There is currently no means of reserving a campsite, except for group camping in Sheep Pass and Indian Cove. There is currently no charge for most camping in the park, although there are plans to charge for campsites in the future. Many climbers stay in Hidden Valley Campground. Hidden Valley is near many fine climbs and close to most other major climbing areas. Other campgrounds are, in preferential order: Ryan, Jumbo, Belle and Indian Cove. Indian Cove is generally warmer, but is isolated from most other climbing areas. There is a 14 day per year camping limit in the park. If planning a long stay, make alternative camping arrangements. There is virtually no formal car camping areas outside the park. The sole exception is Knott's Sky Park in 29 Palms (which is primarily a RV park). Rates are approximately $7.50 per day.

ABOUT THE ROCK

The rock formations at Joshua Tree tend to be dome-like, and in most cases are surrounded by flat sandy washes and open plains. Some of the rock formations in fact, are no more than a huge pile of stacked boulders. Many formations have a number of boulders around their base which can offer numerous, excellent boulder problems. There are many established bouldering spots and problems. Mari Gingery's *Joshua Tree Bouldering* and Craig Fry's *Southern California Bouldering Guide* are excellent references for Joshua Tree bouldering.

Joshua Tree rock is granite in origin, of a type called quartz monzonite. Due to the particular way the rock has cooled and was subsequently weathered, the rock is generally quite rough in texture. This means the rock is highly climbable and care is needed to avoid cuts and scrapes. Steep faces often have "plates" which may provide large hand holds.

The cracks at Joshua Tree are plentiful, and vary from shallow and flared to clean and split. Camming devices are extremely helpful (and often necessary). Generally, the western faces of the rock formations tend to be lower angled and rougher in texture. The eastern faces are steeper, often overhanging, and the rock is usually much smoother, even polished. Crystallin and other intrusion dikes crisscross many of the formations and provide for numerous excellent traversing and vertical face climbs.

It is not uncommon for the rock at Joshua Tree to vary considerably in quality. It can range from quite grainy and even loose, to extremely high quality and smooth. Certain areas in the park are known for poor rock; other areas have mostly excellent rock.

EQUIPMENT

Joshua Tree has a mix of "traditional" and "sport" routes. Gear is often needed for protection and/or anchors, even for bolted face routes. If you are used to climbing exclusively on sport routes, remember that even fully bolted face climbs at Joshua Tree may not have "sport" type protection. It may be possible to take long falls. A standard Joshua Tree rack would consist of camming devices 0.5 through 3 inches, small to medium wired nuts (0.25 inch to 0.75 inch), micro-nuts (brass-steel), and an assortment of Quickdraws and runners. This guide often lists general protection requirements for each route, but you must be the judge of how much gear you need to safely protect a climb.

FOOD, WATER AND SHOWERS

There is no water or food available in the park. Stock up before entering the park or have a car at your disposal for this purpose. Joshua Tree, Yucca Valley and 29 Palms have well-stocked supermarkets. Additionally, these towns have sprouted a virtual swarm of reasonably priced restaurants, as well as "fast food" places. The most popular place to shower is The Sands Motel in Yucca Valley. Showers, towel and private room for changing are $3.00. The Sands Motel is located at 55446 29 Palms Highway (Hwy. 62) Yucca Valley. The Sand's telephone number is: 619-365-4615.

CAMPFIRES

If you desire an evening campfire, bring wood with you (it can also be purchased in town). No natural vegetation (dead or not) may be gathered for burning or any other purpose in the park. The desert environment depends upon natural decay of plant life; the removal of it by visitors is damaging to the delicate balance of life. In addition to being an environmentally unsound practice, it is illegal; you can be cited by the rangers and fined.

MOTEL ACCOMMODATIONS

Many climbers who travel long distances to the park for short visits may find all the campgrounds are full, or may not have all their camping gear with them. Climbers commonly stay in one of the many reasonably priced motels in the Joshua Tree and Yucca Valley area. The following motels are recommended and welcome climbers' business:

OASIS OF EDEN MOTEL
56377 29 Palms Highway
Yucca Valley, CA 92284
(619)365-6321
60 Rooms, pool, continental breakfast
Rates: $34.75 to $49.75

DESERT VIEW MOTEL
57471 Primrose Drive
Yucca Valley, CA 92284
(619)365-9706
14 Rooms, pool, kitchenettes, in-room coffee, HBO
Rates: $35.50 to $45.50

YUCCA SUPER 8 MOTEL
57096 29 Palms Highway
Yucca Valley, CA 92284
(619)228-1773 (800)800-8000
48 Rooms, pool, HBO, group discounts
Rates: $34.88 to $42.88

YUCCA INN
7500 Camino Del Cielo
Yucca Valley, CA 92284
(619)365-3311
74 Rooms, pool, three jacuzzis, climber's discount
Rates: $35.09 to $49.98

THE SANDS MOTEL
55446 29 Palms Highway
Yucca Valley, CA 92284
(619)365-4615
12 Rooms, cable TV, free HBO, phones, climber's discount
Rates: $25.00 to 35.00 single

OFF-ROAD TRAVEL

The use of mountain bikes (or any vehicles) off established roads is prohibited. When walking, stay on marked trails and use only consolidated and established footpaths where possible. Climbers can also minimize their impact by walking in sandy wash areas whenever possible.

RATINGS

All the climbs listed in this guide are given a difficulty rating, and where applicable, a quality and/or protection rating.

The difficulty rating system used in this guidebook is the Tahquitz Decimal System, (also known as the Yosemite Decimal System–YDS) which is used throughout the United States. Climbers may find the ratings at Joshua Tree harder or easier than what they are accustomed to, and the ratings given for some routes may just be wrong. Keep this in mind, take the ratings with

International Rating Systems Compared

German	YDS	British		Australian	French
	5.0				
	5.1				
	5.2				
	5.3				
	5.4				
	5.5				
	5.6				
5+	5.7	4b	VS		5a
6-	5.8	4c		15	5b
6	5.9		HVS	16 / 17	5c
6+	5.10a	5a		18	6a
7-	5.10b	5b	E1	19	6a+
7	5.10c		E2	20	6b
7+	5.10d			21	6b+
	5.11a	5c			6c
8-	5.11b		E3	22	
8	5.11c			23	6c+
8+	5.11d	6a	E4	24	7a
9-	5.12a			25	7a+
9	5.12b		E5	26	7b
	5.12c	6b		27	7b+
9+	5.12d			28	7c
10-	5.13a	6c	E6		7c+
10	5.13b			29	8a
	5.13c	7a		30	8a+
10+	5.13d		E7	31	8b
11-	5.14a			32	8b+

a grain of salt (or granite) and use your own judgement. A rating comparison chart is included to assist foreign climbers in determining the relative difficulty of the climbs listed.

A "star" or "quality" rating is used in this guide. Climbs are given no stars if they are considered just average or less in quality and one through three stars (on an ascending scale) if they are thought to be better routes.

In this guidebook "R" and "X" ratings are given to some routes. This guide does not use either the G or PG protection ratings. The protection ratings in this guide are **NOT** intended to tell you that a climb is well protected; you should **NEVER** presume that a route **NOT** given a R or X rating is well protected.

ABOUT TRASH, POOT SLINGS AND OTHER FORMS OF POLLUTION

Climbers can have a measurable impact on the delicate desert environment and bear the responsibility to lessen this impact. Trash is one of the most tangible forms of environmental impact and takes many forms including: discarded (used) tape, improperly disposed of human waste (including toilet paper), and nylon slings left on the rock.

Pick up all trash you encounter (even if you didn't leave it!) Use toilets whenever possible, even if it means a short walk or drive. Where toilets are not available, **DO NOT** leave human waste anywhere near waterways (i.e., dry stream beds) or on/near trails. Although many climbers make the habit of burying their waste, the fact remains that in desert areas human waste decomposes the quickest when not buried. Soiled paper should be carried out in a small plastic zip locked bag. This is the only way to insure that the dry desert environment does not have to struggle for years to decompose it on its own.

Avoid leaving slings behind. When necessary, leave only natural (rock colored) webbing. **Do NOT** tie slings directly into bolts. Looping a sling through the eye is just as safe and allows subsequent parties to easily remove it. Brightly colored bolt hangers (as opposed to natural colored bolt hangers) can be highly visible and they have been banned in the park since 1989, **Buy only bolt hangers which blend with the natural rock color.**

ABOUT CHIPPING, GLUING AND BOLTING

It is currently illegal in the park to use motorized (electric) drills to place bolts. It is also illegal throughout the National Park System to chip holds or use glue to add or reinforce a hold. In an unprecedented and unjustified move, the park has banned all bolting and replacement in designated wilderness areas (83%) of the park. If you are injured in a fall resulting from

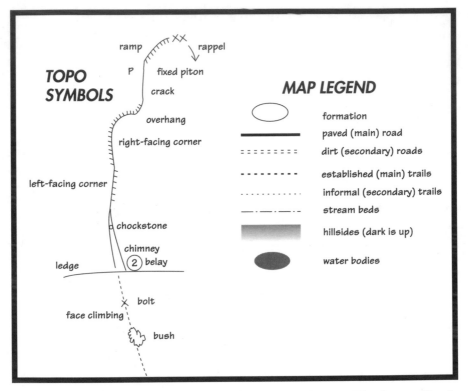

a failed bolt, report this to either Friends of Joshua Tree or The Access Fund **IMMEDIATELY.**

HOW TO USE THIS GUIDE

This guide is arranged in the order that you would encounter rock formations as you drive into the park from the Joshua Tree (west) entrance. Indian Cove is listed last. For nearly every area in this book, there is an overview map showing the various rock formations. There should always be a reference in the guide to the closest map that covers the area in question. In most cases detailed topos or photos are used for identification of formations as well as specific routes. In some cases only verbal descriptions are used. The maps, verbal descriptions, topos and/or photographs should be used together in order to locate routes. If "right" or "left" is used, this refers to the direction as though you were facing the cliff.

CORRECTIONS

Sometimes the information provided in this guidebook may not be entirely clear or may have inaccuracies. Please send any corrections to this information to the author at: PO Box 4554, Laguna Beach, CA 92652. All corrections and suggestions are welcome.

HISTORY

Joshua Tree has a relatively long and interesting climbing history. Many top climbers have visited Joshua Tree and left their mark in the many fine climbs that exist. Joshua Tree's early climbing days are shrouded in mystery. Little is known about the period from 1940 through the early 1960s, when Joshua's climbing was in its infancy. It is known that local hardmen such as Royal Robbins, TM Herbert, Mark Powell, Eric Beck, Tom Frost and others frequented the park during this time frame. For the most part activity was limited to times when poor weather kept the more alpine areas (Tahquitz and Yosemite) closed. Joshua Tree was considered merely a "practice area." Unfortunately, no one took the climbing seriously enough to record route names or first ascent parties. It is known, however, that many of the obvious cracks in the Hidden Valley Campground area were free climbed in the late 50s and early 60s.

From the mid 60s to the beginning of the 70s, several new groups of climbers "discovered" Joshua Tree. The predominant group, "The Desert Rats," included Woody Stark, Dick Webster, John Wolfe, Bill Briggs, Dick James, Al Ruiz, Howard Weamer and others. The Desert Rats were generally unaware of their predecessors' accomplishments, and free climbing standards were years (if not decades) behind most of the country. Most of the major lines in Hidden Valley Campground were climbed during this time frame. In 1970 the first "official" guidebook was published; most routes were 5.7 or under and aid was in common use. The appearance of the guidebook did focus more attention on the park and climbing began to experience a boom.

In the early 70s, climbers such a Richard Harrison, Rick Accomazzo, John Long, Tobin Sorenson, Jim Wilson and John Bachar brought high free climbing standards to Joshua Tree. In two short years (1970 to 1972), the most difficult routes went from 5.9 to 5.11. Development also began to intensify outside the campground, and areas like Saddle Rocks, Hall of Horrors, and the Rusty Wall saw development. Classics of the early 70s include **Illusion Dweller** (5.10b, 1973), the **Exorcist** (5.10a, 1974), **Hyperion Arch** (5.11c, 1974), **O'Kelley's Crack** (5.10c) and **Wanger Banger** (5.11c).

By the mid and late 70s, exploration of the park began in earnest. People began to look to look at the vast route potential in the Wonderland of Rocks. Climbers "discovered" the Astrodomes and, within a few short years, established classics such as **Solid Gold** (5.10a), **Such a Savage** (5.11a) and **Figures on a Landscape** (5.10b). Most of climbs established in the park from the late 70s through the early 80s were accomplished by only a few groups of individuals and a handful of climbers.

Since about the mid 80s, an increasing number of climbers have established new routes at the park. Difficulty standards also began to take a big leap in the mid to late 80s and early 90s. There are a large number of 5.12 and harder routes in the park, including several unrepeated routes in the 5.13d/14a range. Tremendous new areas, such as Queen Mountain and Oz, were also discovered and development continues to this day.

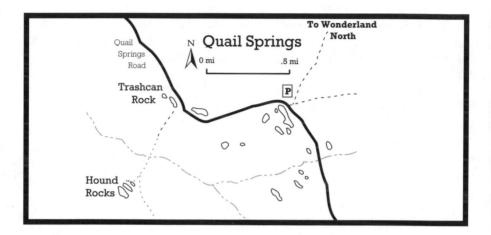

THE ROUTES

TRASHCAN ROCK (Quail Springs Picnic Area)

Trashcan Rock is the first formation of major importance encountered on the drive into the park from the town of Joshua Tree. A paved parking area, picnic table and bathroom are found here, but no camping is allowed. The Park Service has designated this area for day-use only. This is a fine beginners' area. Trashcan Rock is located on the right (west) side of the road, approximately 6 miles from the park entrance. This area also serves as parking for Hound Rocks and The White Cliffs of Dover, located to the southwest.

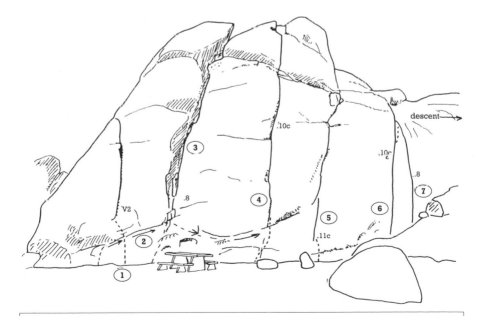

TRASHCAN ROCK (QUAIL SPRINGS PICNIC AREA) EAST FACE

1 Ripper (11 V2) ★
2 Gripper Traverse (10 V0+)
3 Wallaby Crack (8)
4 Hermanutic (10c R) ★
5 Butterfly Crack (11c) ★★
6 Left Sawdust Crack (10c)
7 Right Sawdust Crack (8) ★

EAST FACE

Easiest descent is off the north end of the formation.

1   **Ripper (11 V2)** ★   Boulder problem, but gets sort of high off the deck.

2   **Gripper Traverse (10 V0+)**   Boulder problem traverse.

3   **Wallaby Crack (8)**   Pro: To 3 inches.

4   **Hermanutic (10c R)** ★   Thin and hard to protect at crux. Pro: Mostly small to 2 inches.

5   **Butterfly Crack (11c)** ★★   The classic on the formation. Start with a boulder problem-like crux at the bottom, which leads to easier (5.9) climbing. Pro: Small wired nuts to 2.5 inches.

6   **Left Sawdust Crack (10c)**   Usually toproped; crux at the top. Pro: Small to 2 inches.

7   **Right Sawdust Crack (8)** ★   Hand crack. Pro: Medium to 2.5 inches.

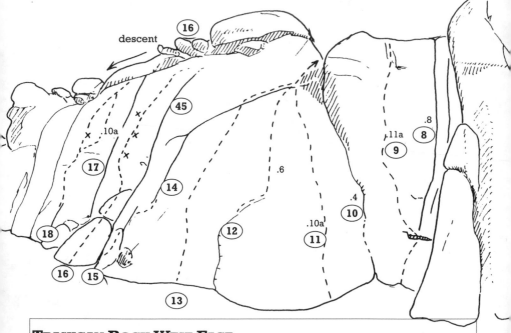

TRASHCAN ROCK WEST FACE			
8	Cranny (8) ★	14	Walkway (4 R)
9	History (11a TR)	15	B-1 (1)
10	Eschar (4)	16	Tiptoe (7+) ★
11	Bimbo (10a R/X)	17	B-2 (3)
12	Tulip (6 R/X)	18	Profundity (10a or 5.10c)
13	Baby-Point-Five (8 R/X)		

WEST FACE

Many of the face routes (with exception of Tiptoe and Profundity) are unprotected and usually toproped. Descend off the north end of the rock.

8   **Cranny**   **(8)** ★   A fun route up double cracks. Pro: To 2 inches.

9   **History**   **(11a TR)**   Climb the face between **Cranny** and **Eschar**.

10   **Eschar**   **(4)**   Pro: Medium to 2.5 inches.

11   **Bimbo**   **(10a R/X)**   Crux at the bottom. Pro: Either toprope or climb with no pro.

12   **Tulip**   **(6 R/X)**   Runout with little pro.

13   **Baby-Point-Five**   **(8 R/X)**   Hard entry moves (unprotected) to easy crack-ramp.

14   **Walkway**   **(4 R)**   Unprotected crux at bottom.

15   **B-1**   **(1)**   Pro: To 3 inches.

16   **Tiptoe**   **(7+)** ★   Fun route past three bolts.

17   **B-2**   **(3)**   Pro: To 3 inches.

18   **Profundity**   **(10a or 10c)** Two bolts. Going straight up past the bolt is more difficult than going slightly right, then up.

HOUND ROCKS

These rocks are located approximately 0.5 mile (0.8 km) southwest of Trashcan Rock. Park at the Trashcan Rock parking area and follow a rough trail to this area. The routes lie on the eastern faces of two principal rock formations. See map page 10.

BASKERVILLE ROCK

The first (and smaller) of the Hound Rocks to be encountered is Baskerville Rock. Baskerville Rock is actually two rocks; all the routes lie on the larger left-hand rock. The following routes lie on the east face. Descend (easy class 5) off back (west) side, behind Right Baskerville Crack.

19   **Left Baskerville Crack**   **(10b R)**   Face climb up to the wide crack near the center of the east face. An awkward start and wide, hard-to-protect portions above do not make this a popular choice. Pro: To 5 inches

20   **Don't Bolt Me**   **(11b TR)** ★   Steep face climbing five feet left of Right Baskerville Crack. Pro: Nuts for anchors.

21   **Right Baskerville Crack**   **(10a)** ★★   The steep thin crack 20 feet right of Left Baskerville Crack, on the right side of the main face. The classic climb in this area, on good rock. Pro: Small to 2 inches.

HOUND ROCK

This is the larger of the two main formations and has several good cracks on the east face. The base is located in a small gully. Easiest descent is down the south end of the formation.

22   **Direct Wrench (11a TR)**

23   **Crescent Wrench (10d)** ★   Pro: Many thin to 1.5 inches.

24   **An Eye to The West (9)** ★   Pro: Medium to 2.5 inches.

25   **Tossed Green (10a)** ★★   A good crack outing. Rap from anchor/slings. Pro: Many to 2.5 inches.

26   **White Powder (7)**   Pro: to 3.5 inches

27   **Over The Hill (9)**   Pro: To 3 inches

28   **Animalitos (11b)** ★   Commonly toproped. Pro: Many small to 2.5 inches.

29   **Animalargos (11c R)** ★★   Most people toprope this climb. Pro: Good variety of small to 3 inches.

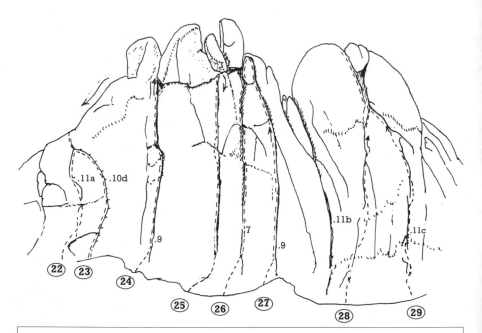

HOUND ROCK

22	Direct Wrench *(11a TR)*	26	White Powder *(7)*
23	Crescent Wrench *(10d)* ★	27	Over The Hill *(9)*
24	An Eye to The West *(9)* ★	28	Animalitos *(11b)* ★
25	Tossed Green *(10a)* ★★	29	Animalargos *(11c R)* ★★

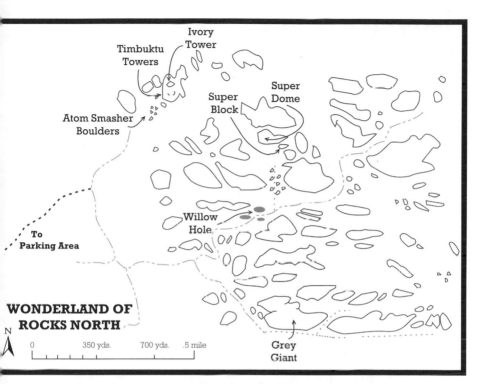

Ivory
Tower

Timbuktu
Towers

Super
Dome

Super
Block

Atom Smasher
Boulders

To
Parking Area

Willow
Hole

WONDERLAND OF
ROCKS NORTH

N

0   350 yds.   700 yds.   .5 mile

Grey
Giant

WONDERLAND OF ROCKS NORTH

The Wonderland of Rocks is a huge and remote concentration of rock formations bounded by Indian Cove to the north, Barker Dam to the south, Key's Ranch to the west and Queen Mountain to the east. Due to its vast size, there are two main points of entry and routes are described in two different sections. The northern section (Wonderland North) is described in the following section (see map for coverage). The southern section (Wonderland South) is described near the Barker Dam section of this guide.

APPROACH: Park at Key's Corner (a sharp right turn in the road 0.7 mile (1.1 km) east of Trashcan Rock; approximately. 6.7 miles from the park entrance). Take a trail (the Wonderland Trail) that heads northeast from the Key's Corner parking lot. After about one mile, it joins a larger north-south trail (the Old Trail). Head north, after 350 yards, you will pass the junction with the Indian Cove hiking trail (don't take the Indian Cove Trail), continue curving northeast for 1.5 miles to where the trail ends in a sandy wash (the Sandy Wash Junction).

THE ATOM SMASHERS

From the Sandy Wash Junction (see APPROACH above) head roughly straight ahead (northeast) toward a group of angular-shaped boulders and formations which can be seen about 700 yards ahead. Although the main wash now heads south, you are following a narrow stream bed northeast until you reach an open basin. The main Atom Smashers area lies directly ahead. Map, page 15.

TIMBUKTU TOWERS

The large (main) formations on the hillside are referred to as the Timbuktu Towers. The largest formation has many routes on the west and south faces. The large, leaning pillar high on the north side of the Timbuktu Towers is the Ivory Tower.

30   **Sine Wave (9)** ★ (one bolt)   Pro: Thin to 2 inches.

31   **Gravity Waves (11c/d)** ★★   Route was originally rated 5.11a, but a big hold has broken and it is apparently much harder now. Pro: Bolts, thin to 2 inches.

32   **Gravity Works (11c)** ★★   Pro: Bolts, thin to 2 inches.

33   **Offshoot (10b)**   Pro: To 3.5 inches.

34   **The Bates Motel (12b)** ★★   Pro: Six bolts, thin to 2 inches.

35   **Polytechnics (10c)** ★   Three bolts on the wall to the left of Psychokenesis.

36   **Nuclear Waste (9+)**   This route is the off width crack about 50 feet left of Psychokenesis.

37   **Psychokenesis (11b)** ★   Climb an overhanging thin crack/ramp to the upper dihedral. Two pitches.

38   **Psychotechnics (11b)** ★   This route allows for a better second-pitch alternative to Psychokenesis. Climb that route, and belay where the upper dihedral eases in difficulty. Climb right, out of the dihedral, then up the exposed arête past a bolt to the top.

THE IVORY TOWER

This is the obvious, leaning pillar above and right (northeast) of the west face of Timbuktu Towers. The following four sport routes, including the yet unrepeated La Machine, lie on its overhanging north face.

39   **The Powers That Be (13a)** ★★★   This route has five bolts and is near the left edge of the face.

40   **Chain of Addiction (13c)** ★★★   Climb the center of the face past nine bolts.

41   **Ocean of Doubt (13b/c)** ★★★   This route is just right of Chain of Addiction.

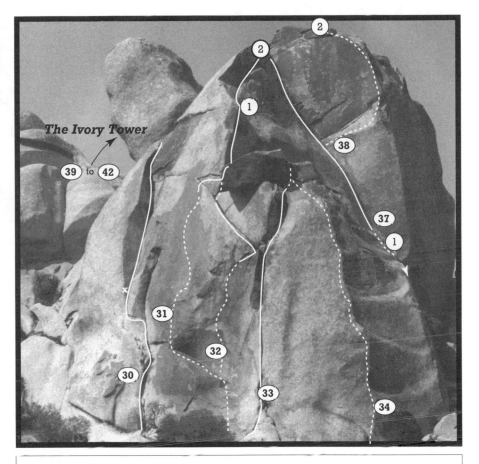

TIMBUKTU TOWERS

30	Sine Wave (9) @ (1 bolt)		35	Polytechnics (10c) ★
31	Gravity Waves (11c/d) ★★		36	Nuclear Waste (9+)
32	Gravity Works (11c) ★★		37	Psychokenesis (11b)★
33	Offshoot (10b)		38	Psychotechnics (11b) ★
34	The Bates Motel (12b) ★★			

    42   La Machine (13d) ★★★   This route is near the right edge and has six bolts.

ATOM SMASHER BOULDERS

These boulders lie about 125 yards south-southeast and down the hill from the main Timbuktu Towers formation. The boulders are generally about 50 feet high. Many face climbs are found on the sharp arêtes. Map page 15.

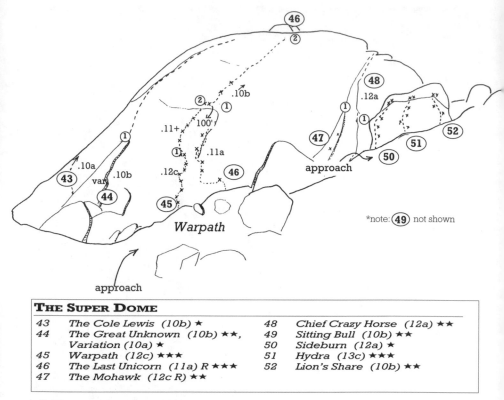

*note: (49) not shown

Warpath

approach

THE SUPER DOME

43	The Cole Lewis (10b) ★		48	Chief Crazy Horse (12a) ★★
44	The Great Unknown (10b) ★★,		49	Sitting Bull (10b) ★★
	Variation (10a) ★		50	Sideburn (12a) ★
45	Warpath (12c) ★★★		51	Hydra (13c) ★★★
46	The Last Unicorn (11a) R ★★★		52	Lion's Share (10b) ★★
47	The Mohawk (12c R) ★★			

THE SUPER DOME

From the Sandy Wash Junction (see APPROACH, page 15) turn south following the main wash. After about 450 yards continue in the wash where it curves to the east. Stay in the main wash as it winds roughly eastward for about 0.5 miles until you reach an open area with several large ponds of water. This is Willow Hole an important watering area for wildlife. From Willow Hole, walk about 200 yards east along Rattlesnake Canyon over a rise and down into an open area. A narrow rock-filled canyon heading north leads to the base of the obvious and beautiful Super Dome. Descent is either several rappels or walk off to the northeast. See map page 15.

43   The Cole Lewis (10b) ★   Start up the left variation of the next route, but head out right after 40 feet or so. Pro: Bolts and gear to 2 inches.

44   The Great Unknown (10b) ★★   Take the right crack system which leads to face climbing. Pro: Bolts and gear to 2 inches. Variation (10a) ★   Take the crack in the left corner up to the face.

45   Warpath (12c) ★★★   An excellent multi-pitch sport route in a remote setting. Pro: Sport route requiring only draws.

46 **The Last Unicorn (11a R) ★★★** One of the classic routes of Joshua, but the remote locale and reputation for bold climbing puts many people off. Pro: A few thin to medium, slings.

47 **The Mohawk (12c R) ★★** Runout at top. Pro: Thin to medium.

48 **Chief Crazy Horse (12a) ★★** First pitch Runout (10b). Pro: Thin to medium.

49 **Sitting Bull (10b) ★★** This is a classic finger-to-fist crack in a corner on the southeast side of the dome.

THE SUPER BLOCK

This formation lies immediately to the right of The Super Dome. To approach, start at the base of Chief Crazy Horse. "Third class" (5.6) up the slab to the right to a bolt, then stem out right and traverse around to the south face of the rock. All routes are sport bolted.

50 **Sideburn (12a) ★** Climb over the roof and continue up the southwest arête. This is the left most route on the formation. Pro: Bolts.

51 **Hydra (13c) ★★★** This bolt-protected route leads up to the crest of the "wave-like" face to the right of Sideburn. Pro: Bolts.

52 **Lion's Share (10b) ★★** This route climbs the arête to the right of Hydra. Pro: Bolts.

GREY GIANT

From Sandy Wash Junction (see APPROACH, page 15) turn south following the main wash. After about 450 yards continue in the wash where it curves to the east. Stay in the main wash as it winds roughly eastward for about 375 yards, then take the second side wash to the right (heading roughly south). The Grey Giant can just be seen several hundred yards to the southeast of this point. Follow this wash in a southeasterly direction until rock scrambling leads to the west end of the Grey Giant. See map page 15.

53 **Illusion (7)** Pro: To 3 inches..

54 **Transfusion (12a) ★★** Pro: Mostly thin to 3 inches.

55 **Lithophiliac (11a) ★★** Pro: Mostly thin to 3 inches.

56 **Hyperion (11c) ★★★** One of the all-time Joshua Tree classics. A short technical crux and loads of great climbing. Pro: Thin and many .5 to 4 inches.

57 **Janus (var.) (10d) ★** A variation to upper pitches of Hyperion.

58 **Vortex (var.) (10b) ★** Another variation to Hyperion.

59 **The DMB (9) ★** Pro: Three bolts, two-bolt anchor/rap.

60 **Two Left Feet (9) ★** Pro: Medium to 2 inches, one bolt.

61 **Dawn Yawn (11d) ★★** Pro: Thin to 2 inches.

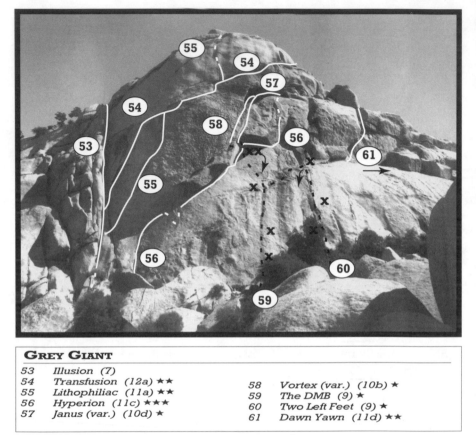

GREY GIANT

53	Illusion (7)		
54	Transfusion (12a) ★★	58	Vortex (var.) (10b) ★
55	Lithophiliac (11a) ★★	59	The DMB (9) ★
56	Hyperion (11c) ★★★	60	Two Left Feet (9) ★
57	Janus (var.) (10d) ★	61	Dawn Yawn (11d) ★★

LOST HORSE VALLEY WEST

These formations lie to the west of Hemingway Buttress and are approached from the dirt road leading to Lost Horse Ranger Station (Ranger Station Road). The Ranger Station Road is located on the west side of Quail Springs Road. See map page22.

LOST HORSE WALL

Take the Ranger Station Road west for .5 mile to a small parking area on the south (left). The large Lost Horse Wall lies several hundred yards south of the road, on the east side of a large valley. It faces west and receives good afternoon sun, although it is subject to the wind. To descend, walk off to the right (south) down slabs and boulders. For all these routes, scramble (Class 3) up onto a ledge system from the left, then traverse right to the base of the climb.

    62   **The Swift (7)** ★★   A good easy multi-pitch route. Pro: To 2.5 inches.

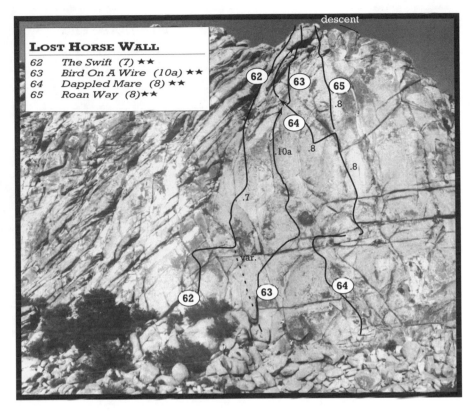

Lost Horse Wall

62	The Swift (7) ★★
63	Bird On A Wire (10a) ★★
64	Dappled Mare (8) ★★
65	Roan Way (8)★★

63　Bird On A Wire (10a) ★★　Pro: Thin to 2.5 inches.

64　Dappled Mare (8) ★★　Pro:Thin to 2 inches.

65　Roan Way (8) ★★　Pro: Thin to 2 inches.

IMAGINARY VOYAGE FORMATION

This formation consists of a 50-foot summit block lying atop a hill which forms the west side of the valley containing the Lost Horse Wall. A large cave/crack is located on its west side (Imaginary Voyage). Park about .6 mile down the Ranger Station Road, near the point the road is closed to further vehicle traffic. Descend off the southeast side. See map, page 22.

66　**Imaginary Voyage (10d) ★★★**　This is the overhanging crack to a roof located in the cave of the west side of the summit block. Pro: 1 to 5 inches.

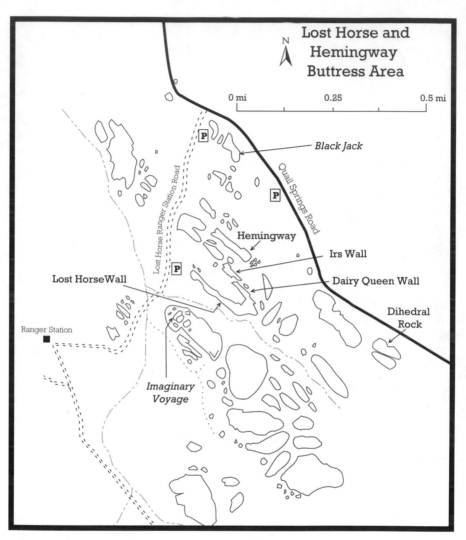

N
Lost Horse and
Hemingway
Buttress Area

0 mi   0.25   0.5 mi

Black Jack

Quail Springs Road

Lost Horse Ranger Station Road

Hemingway

Irs Wall

Lost Horse Wall

Dairy Queen Wall

Dihedral
Rock

Ranger Station

Imaginary
Voyage

HEMINGWAY BUTTRESS AREA

The routes and crags described in this section lie to the south of the junction of Quail Springs Road and the Ranger Station Road, and are all approached from Quail Springs Road.

KEN BLACK BUTTRESS

This formation lies next to Quail Springs Road 300 yards south of the Ranger Station Road and is recognized as a dark colored buttress pointing toward the road. The following climb lies on the southern side of the formation, left of an arête and right of a curving crack/corner system.

67   **Black Jack (10d)** ★★★   The steep face with seven bolts. Sport anchors-lower-offs at top. Pro: Optional 2 to 2.5 inch cam.

HEMINGWAY BUTTRESS

This long formation lies about 250 yards directly west of the Hemingway Parking area. The parking area is located approximately .2 mile south of the Quail Springs-Ranger Station Road junction. The formation has many fine crack climbs on the east face (facing the road). From the parking area follow the marked trail straight west to the base of the cliff. Routes may be accessed by traversing the base of the cliff. There are many descent routes off Hemingway Buttress, largely dependent upon which route you have climbed. A bolted rappel anchor is located just right of the top of White Lightning; two ropes are required. Downclimbs are shown on the topo. See map, page 22.

68   **Overseer (9)** ★★   Climb shallow corner then go right over the roof (easier than it looks). Pro: Thin to 2 inches.

69   **Direct Start (10a R)** ★   Climb discontinuous cracks straight up to roof/bulge of Overseer. Pro: Thin.

70   **White Lightning (7)** ★★   Obvious straight-in crack. Pro: 1 to 3.5 inches.

71   **Poodles Are People Too (10b)** ★★★   This is the very thin crack just right of White Lightning; facing climbing with crack protection. Pro: Many thin to 1.5 inches.

72   **Feltoneon Physics (8)** ★   This thin to hands crack lies immediately left of Prepackaged. Pro: To 2.5 inches.

73   **Prepackaged (10a)** ★★   Take diagonal thin crack which widens over bulge. Pro: Thin to 2.5 inches.

74   **The Importance of Being Ernest (10d R)** ★★   Crux down low leads over roof to very shallow cracks near the top with some dubious fixed copperheads. Pro: Very thin to 2 inches.

75   **Scary Poodles (11b)** ★★   Start up lower crack, switch over to upper crack. Continue past a fixed pin, then up arch at top. Pro: Thin to 1 inch.

76   **Head Over Heals (10a)** ★★   This route lies about 150 feet right of Scary Poodles, on the right-hand arête/corner of the main Hemingway Buttress formation. Climb up a dihedral, traverse left past a bolt and follow a hand crack around the corner to the top. Pro: To 2.5 inches, one bolt.

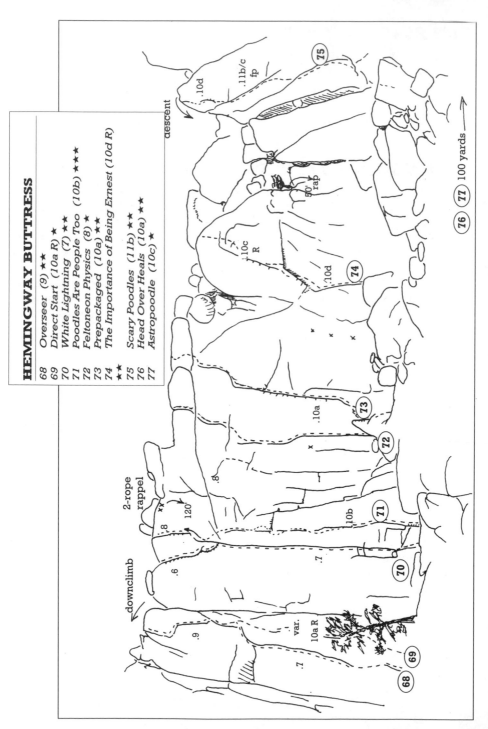

HEMINGWAY BUTTRESS

68   Overseer (9) ★★
69   Direct Start (10a R) ★
70   White Lightning (7) ★★
71   Poodles Are People Too (10b) ★★★
72   Feltoneon Physics (8) ★
73   Prepackaged (10a) ★★
74   The Importance of Being Ernest (10d R) ★★
75   Scary Poodles (11b) ★★
76   Head Over Heals (10a) ★★
77   Astropoodle (10c) ★

77   **Astropoodle (10c)** ★   Do the Head Over Heels roof, then continue straight up to a bolt at the next roof. Work right past another bolt to top.

THE IRS WALL

This formation lies about 75 yards behind and to the left (southwest) of Hemingway Buttress. To approach the rock, follow the marked trail from the Hemingway Parking area until it splits, take the left fork which leads toward the IRS and Dairy Queen Walls. See map, page 22.

78   **Alf's Arête (11a)** ★★   This route lies on the extreme left (southeast) corner of the IRS Wall. Great bolted face climbing up the arête. Pro: Seven bolts.

79   **Tax Man (10a)** ★★★   This is the straight-in thin crack near the right-hand side of the IRS Wall (50 yards right of Alf's Arête). It is clearly visible from the road and is about 100 feet in height. Descend to the right (north) and down a narrow chimney. Pro:Thin to 2.5 inches.

THE IRS WALL

78   *Alf's Arête (11a)* ★★
79   *Tax Man (10a)* ★★★

Dairy Queen Wall, Left

Dairy Queen Wall, Right

DAIRY QUEEN WALL

80	Pat Adams Dihedral (11c) ★★★	85	Chili Dog (10a) ★
81	Toxic Waltz (12a) ★	86	Dilly Bar (5)
82	Scrumdillyishus (7) ★	87	Mr. Misty Kiss (7) ★★
83	Frosty Cone (7) ★★	88	Double Decker (6)
84	Hot Fudge (9 R) ★	89	Nuts and Cherries (6)

DAIRY QUEEN WALL

This formation lies to the left (south) of the IRS Wall and about 150 yards southwest of Hemingway Buttress. From the Hemingway parking area, take the climbers trail to where it splits, head left and follow this toward the rock. Scramble up to the base of the routes. Its right section is very knobby and has several cracks of varying widths. These routes are generally good moderate routes, although protection may be tricky. For this reason they are often toproped. See map page 22.

80   **Pat Adams Dihedral (11c) ★★★**   This obvious, overhanging right-facing dihedral lies high on the formation about 150 feet left of the routes shown in the topo. Pro: Thin to 2 inches.

81   **Toxic Waltz (12a) ★**   This is a five bolt face climb on the arête to the right of Pat Adam's Dihedral. Bring nuts for anchors.

82   **Scrumdillyishus (7) ★**

83   Frosty Cone (7) ★★
84   Hot Fudge (9 R) ★
85   Chili Dog (10a) ★   Pro: Small wires to 2 inches.
86   Dilly Bar (5)
87   Mr. Misty Kiss (7) ★★
88   Double Decker (6)
89   Nuts and Cherries (6)

DIHEDRAL ROCK

This formation lies on the west side of the Quail Springs Road, about ?? mile from Hidden Valley Campground, and .8 mile south of Ranger Station Road junction with Quail Springs Road. The large, left-facing dihedral on its left side can be seen easily from the road. See map, page 22.

90   **Coarse and Buggy (11a/b)** ★★★   This routes goes up the obvious left-facing dihedral. Pro: Many thin to 2 inches.

91   **Sow Sickle (11d)** ★★   This route lies on the right side of the east face, about 50 feet right of Coarse and Buggy, face climbing up to a thin crack. Pro: Bolts, fixed pins and small to medium nuts.

THE REAL HIDDEN VALLEY AREA

Just before the Hidden Valley Campground (just before!), is a road that heads southwest from the Quail Springs Road. This road leads to the Real Hidden Valley. At the end of the paved section of the Real Hidden Valley Road is a parking area. The entrance to the Real Hidden Valley is to the north: a sign and trail marker make this obvious. A Nature Trail makes a loop circuit of Real Hidden Valley. Reference is made to this trail in describing the locations of various formations.

PITTED ROCK

This large formation is to the right of the trail into the Real Hidden Valley. It is northwest of and directly faces the parking area. From the parking area scramble up boulders to reach the base. See map, page 28

92   **Pitfall (11c)** ★   This is a four-bolt face climb on the steep (brown) south face of Pitted Rock, facing the parking area.

93   **Pit Slut (12a)** ★   This is around the corner (east face of Pitted Rock), about 60 feet right of Pitfall. A thin crack leads to a slightly overhanging face. It may be more easily approached from the vicinity of Sports Challenge Rock. Pro: Three bolts, thin to 3 inches. No fixed anchors.

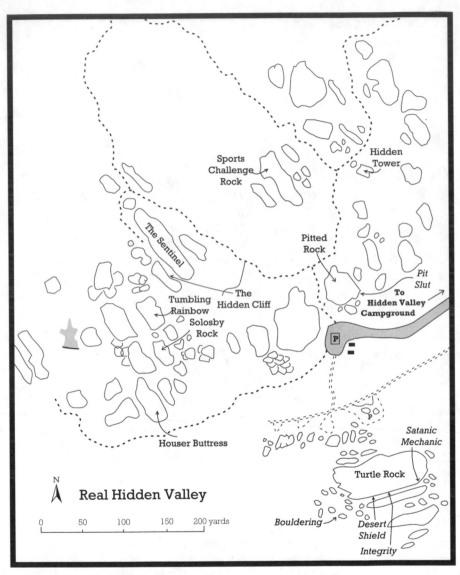

Sports
Challenge
Rock

Hidden
Tower

The Sentinel

Pitted
Rock

Pit
Slut

The
Hidden Cliff

Tumbling
Rainbow
Solosby
Rock

To
Hidden Valley
Campground

P

Houser Buttress

Satanic
Mechanic

N

Real Hidden Valley

Turtle Rock

0   50   100   150   200 yards

Bouldering

Desert
Shield

Integrity

SPORTS CHALLENGE ROCK

*This excellent formation lies roughly in the central part of the Real Hidden
Valley, and is one of the best (and most popular) rock formations in this area.
Most routes on Sports Challenge Rock are easily (and commonly) toproped,
though almost all may be led. From the parking lot, follow the nature trail into
Real Hidden Valley. From here, the west face of Sports Challenge Rock will
be seen about 100 yards to the northeast. See map.*

SPORTS CHALLENGE ROCK WEST FACE

94	Sphincter Quits (9) ★	98	Don't Be Nosey (10d TR)
95	What's It To You (10d) ★★	99	None of Your Business (10b R) ★
96	Rap Bolters Are Weak (12a) ★★	100	Eddie Haskel Takes Manhattan
97	Ride A Wild Bago (10a) ★		(10b R)

SPORTS CHALLENGE ROCK—WEST FACE

94   **Sphincter Quits (9)** ★   Pro: To 2 inches.

95   **What's It To You (10d)** ★★   Use the first bolt of Rap Bolters Are Weak to protect the initial traverse. Pro: Thin to 1.5 inches.

96   **Rap Bolters Are Weak (12a)** ★★   Pro: Four bolts, to 3 inches for anchors.

97   **Ride A Wild Bago (10a)** ★   Pro: To 3 inches.

98   **Don't Be Nosey (10d TR)**

99   **None of Your Business (10b R)** ★   Pro: To 2 inches.

100   **Eddie Haskel Takes Manhattan (10b R)** ★   Pro: Two bolts, thin to 1.5 inches.

SPORTS CHALLENGE ROCK—EAST FACE

The east face is continuously overhanging and has many excellent crack and face climbs. Excellent boulder problems are located on the face just below Leave It To Beaver.

downclimb (4th class)

.10a

descent

.12a

.11c

.10c

.11c/d

(101)

(104) (102)

(105)

(103)

SPORTS CHALLENGE ROCK EAST FACE

101 Clean and Jerk (10c) ★★★	*104 Lobster Lieback (B1+ V5)*
102 Leave It To Beaver (12a) ★★★	*105 Kirkatron B1 (V2)*
103 Cool But Concerned (11d) ★★	

---

101 Clean and Jerk (10c) ★★★   The start is the crux, a good spot is helpful to prevent a ground fall until the crack is reached. Pro: To 3 inches.

102 Leave It To Beaver (12a) ★★★   Most people toprope this route, although reasonable natural protection is available. Pro: To 4 inches.

103 Cool But Concerned (11d) ★★   This route starts about five feet right of the obvious off width crack 25 feet right of Leave It To Beaver. Follow a thin seam/crack to a horizontal, traverse right to a crack leading to the top. Pro: Many small to 1.5 inches.

SPORTS CHALLENGE BOULDERING

The following two boulder problems lie below Leave It To Beaver.

104 Lobster Lieback B1+ (V5)   This is the lieback up curvy, right-facing flakes just right of the obvious tree.

105 Kirkatron B1 (V2)   This is the traverse starting just right of Lobster Lieback and leading to the off width crack 25 feet to the right.

HIDDEN TOWER

This small tower is to the east of Sports Challenge Rock and just east of the Nature Trail. Take the right-hand fork in the Nature Trail, over a wooden bridge. A short distance farther, the trail heads straight north, the formation lies directly to your east. Hike to the left (north) of the formation to get to the east face routes. The formation also can be reached easily from Quail Springs Road. See map, page 28.

106 **Wild Wind (9)** ★ This is the left-hand crack of two cracks on the northeast face of Hidden Tower. Pro: Thin to 2 inches.

107 **Sail Away (8-)** ★★★ This is the right-hand crack of two cracks on the northeast face of Hidden Tower. Pro: To 2 inches.

THE SENTINEL

This large formation lies on the west side of the Real Hidden Valley and sports two large faces. Take the nature trail into Real Hidden Valley and take the left hand fork of the Nature Trail (northwest). The formation is located left of the Nature Trail. The following routes are located on the west face. The easiest approach is to follow the Nature Trail just past the east face, then cut off to the

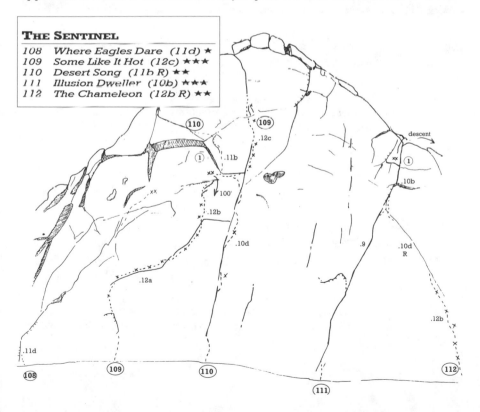

THE SENTINEL

108 *Where Eagles Dare (11d)* ★
109 *Some Like It Hot (12c)* ★★★
110 *Desert Song (11b R)* ★★
111 *Illusion Dweller (10b)* ★★★
112 *The Chameleon (12b R)* ★★

TUMBLING RAINBOW
FORMATION

115	Run For Your Life (10b) ★★★
116	Tonic Boom (12d) ★
117	Tic Tic Boom (12a) ★★
118	Rainy Day, Dream Away (11b R) ★
119	Fisticuffs (10b) ★★

left (west) over a few small boulders, then follow a well used trail running
back south into a canyon. Routes ending on the ledge below the large roof
require two ropes to descend. See map, page 28.

108   **Where Eagles Dare (11d)** ★   This route starts about 65 feet right
of the start of the following climb, in a short, vertical, thin crack, that
is a technical lieback that leads to a right diagonaling crack. This
crack then leads to the left side of a large roof. Pro: Several thin to
2.5 inches.

109   **Some Like It Hot (12c)** ★★★   The first pitch is (12b). Pro: Eight
bolts; The second pitch is (12c). Pro: To 3 inches, four bolts. one-
hundred-foot-plus rap from end of first pitch.

110   **Desert Song (11b R)** ★★   First pitch is (10d) and reasonably
protected. Second pitch is scary. Pro: Thin to 3 inches.

111   **Illusion Dweller (10b)** ★★★   Two ropes needed to rap from bolt
anchor, easy walk off up and to the right. Pro: several thin to 3
inches.

112   **The Chameleon (12b R)** ★★   The crux face moves are
reasonably well protected, but the upper diagonal crack is not. Pro:
Five bolts, nuts to 3 inches.

THE HIDDEN CLIFF

This cliff lies directly opposite Illusion Dweller/The Chameleon and farther south, in a narrow canyon/gully area. It is an outstanding face and is cool on hot afternoons. See map, page 28.

113   **Bikini Whale (12b)** ★★★   A classic sport route that climbs knobs and horizontal bands straight up. Stick clip of first bolt may be desirable. Pro: Five bolts, two-bolt anchor.

114   **G String (13d/14a)** ★★   Climb Bikini Whale to a horizontal crack, go left a short distance, then up an extremely tenuous flake/corner and face. Unrepeated. Pro: Eight bolts.

TUMBLING RAINBOW FORMATION

This is the tallest formation in Real Hidden Valley and lies on the far west side. Take the Nature Trail into Real Hidden Valley and then take the left-hand fork of the Nature Trail. After 30 yards or so, turn left into a small wash, follow this until scrambling up boulders takes you to the base. Descend the first four routes by walking off to the left. See map, page 28.

115   **Run For Your Life (10b)** ★★★   Pro: Six bolts, medium nuts for anchor.

116   **Tonic Boom (12d)** ★   Pro: Five bolts, medium nuts for anchor.

117   **Tic Tic Boom (12a)** ★★   Pro: Five bolts, nuts for anchor.

118   **Rainy Day, Dream Away (11b R)** ★   Pro: Thin to 2.5 inches.

119   **Fisticuffs (10b)** ★★   Pro: To 4 inches.

SOLOSBY FACE

This overhanging, knobby, orange-colored face lies to the left (south) of the Tumbling Rainbow Formation and behind a series of blocks that face the trail. The descent from Tumbling Rainbow leads past this face. To reach it from below, scramble up between huge blocks to the left of the Tumbling Rainbow Face. See map, page 28.

120   **Latin Swing (11c)** ★★   This route ascends the center of the face before traversing right to a thin crack   Probably better as a top rope. Pro: Thin to 2 inches, 1 bolt, 2 bolt anchor.

121   **Bebop Tango (11a/b)** ★★★   Climb buckets and holds on the right side of the face. Pro: 4 Bolts, 2 bolt anchor.

TURTLE ROCK

This large formation lies 150 yards south of the main parking area for the Real Hidden Valley. The area to the southwest of Turtle Rock sports some of the best bouldering in Joshua Tree. Many fine (and high off-the-deck) problems are found here. This is the site of the famous So High Boulder. The following four sport routes lie on the south face in a small corridor. Walk around the western end of the rock, pass under the So High Boulder and enter the corridor near at its west end. See map, page 28.

122   **Desert Shield (13a) ★★★**   This excellent climb is the first route encountered upon entering the corridor on the south side of the rock. Seven bolts lead to cold-shut hooks; one rope reaches on lowering. Setting up a top rope requires a belay and/or medium to 3-inch pro and a second rope. An incomplete project lies immediately left of Desert Shield.

123   **Integrity (14a) ★★★**   Starts about 50 feet right of Desert Shield. Climbs up past bolts then traverses right along a horizontal until continuing straight up again. Two incomplete projects lie between Integrity and Desert Shield.

124   **Jesus Lives (12c) ★**   This route and Satanic Mechanic both lie at the far eastern end of the corridor. Both routes start and end in the same place; this route climbs up and left past bolts. Kinda weird and not very popular.

125   **Satanic Mechanic (12b) ★★★**   This fine sport route climbs up and right to a crack/roof, then heads out left and up to sport anchors. One rope lowers. A belay may be necessary to set up a top rope off the fixed biners.

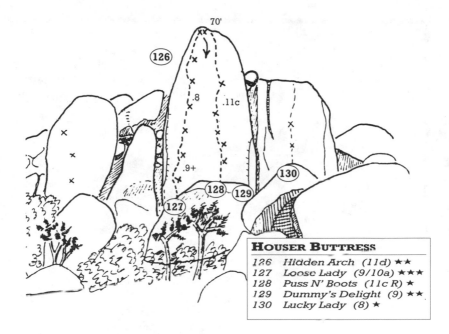

HOUSER BUTTRESS

126	Hidden Arch (11d) ★★
127	Loose Lady (9/10a) ★★★
128	Puss N' Boots (11c R) ★
129	Dummy's Delight (9) ★★
130	Lucky Lady (8) ★

HOUSER BUTTRESS

This prominent buttress of rock is found approximately 225 yards west of the parking picnic area near the northwest corner of Turtle Rock. A trail leads directly to the buttress. See map, page 28.

126   **Hidden Arch (11d)** ★★   Face climb up into a leaning flared dihedral. Pro: Many thin to 2 inches, two bolts, two bolt anchor/rap.

127   **Loose Lady (9/10a)** ★★★   A J-Tree classic for the grade and usually quite popular. Pro: 7 bolts, two bolt anchor/rap.

128   **Puss N' Boots (11c R)** ★   Pro: 7 bolts, two bolt anchor/rap. Bring wired stoppers in case a bolt hanger is missing.

129   **Dummy's Delight (9)** ★★   This is the arching crack around right of the two previous face routes. Pro: To 3 inches.

130   **Lucky Lady (8)** ★   Pro: 2 bolts, to 2 inches.

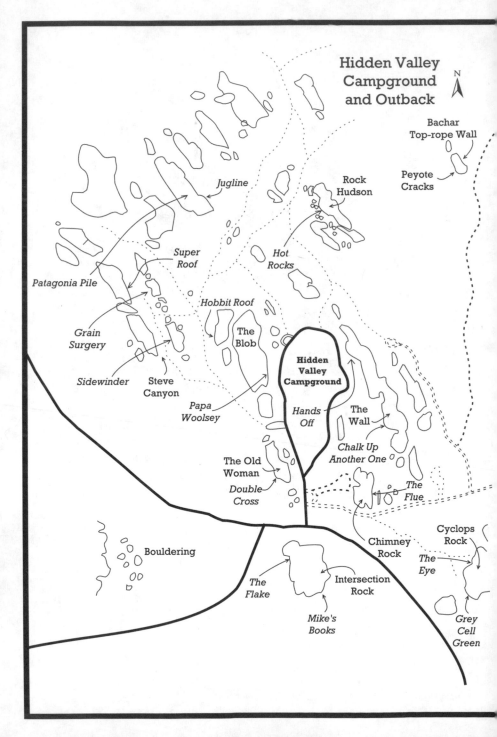

Hidden Valley
Campground
and Outback

N

Bachar
Top-rope Wall

Peyote
Cracks

Rock
Hudson

Jugline

Super
Roof

Hot
Rocks

Patagonia Pile

Hobbit Roof

Grain
Surgery

The
Blob

Hidden
Valley
Campground

Sidewinder   Steve
Canyon

Papa
Woolsey

Hands
Off

The
Wall

Chalk Up
Another One

The Old
Woman

Double
Cross

The
Flue

Cyclops
Rock

Bouldering

Chimney
Rock

The
Eye

The
Flake

Intersection
Rock

Mike's
Books

Grey
Cell
Green

HIDDEN VALLEY CAMPGROUND

This campground is the true center of the Joshua Tree scene. Most climbers camp here, although a 14-day limit can be enforced. The rocks surrounding the campground offer many good to excellent routes. The formation just south of the intersection of Quail Springs Road and the entrance to the campground is Intersection Rock. There is good bouldering along the base and around Intersection Rock. It is described after the route descriptions.

INTERSECTION ROCK – NORTH FACE (facing road)

131 **North Overhang (9) ★★** Belay under overhang, then take the crack out left. Pro: To 2 inches.

132 **Upper Right Ski Track (3) ★** Pro: To 3 inches.

133 **Lower Right Ski Track (10c) ★★** Pro: To 2.5 inches.

134 **Trapeze (11d) ★** Pro: 4 bolts, 1fp and nuts to 2 inches. Variation: Trapeze Left (12c) Climb up to a long roof, move left and go over the roof's left side. Variation: Trapeze Center (12a) Climb over the center of the roof.

135 **Left Ski Track (11a) ★★** Pro: To 3 inches.

136 **Half Track (10a)** After first pitch, continue left and up to easy climbing to top. Pro: Thin to 2 inches.

SOUTH FACE

137 **Mike's Books (6+) ★** This route climbs an obvious and large right-facing dihedral system on the southern part of the rock. Pitch 1. Start to the left and below the dihedral; face climb up and right into the bottom of the dihedral and continue up the corner to a very large ledge (bolt anchors). Pitch 2. Above, climb another dihedral which eventually leads to face climbing past a bolt to a 2 bolt belay/rappel anchor. Rap the route (2 75 foot rappels). Pro: To 3 inches.

WEST FACE

The following two climbs lie just around the corner, to the right, from the North Face.

138 **Overhang Bypass (7) ★★** Walk right from the North Face, around low rocks to a point below the large summit overhang. Pitch 1. Climb shallow crack systems directly up to a small, cave-like overhang, which is passed directly to reach a large sloping ledge beneath the large overhang near the summit (same belay as

INTERSECTION ROCK—NORTH FACE

131	North Overhang (9) ★★		135	Left Ski Track (11a) ★★
132	Upper Right Ski Track (3) ★		136	Half Track (10a)
133	Lower Right Ski Track (10c) ★★		138	Overhang Bypass (7) ★★
134	Trapeze (11d) ★			

North Overhang). Pitch 2. An exciting traverse to the right leads to face climbing past one bolt to the summit. Pro: To 2.5 inches.

139   **The Flake (8) ★**   This route starts about 40 feet right of Overhang Bypass. The bottom of the route is a wide crack-chimney which eventually leads to a thin crack and face climbing. Climb the chimney for 40 feet to a left-facing flake system that ends high on the face (belay possible here). Continue up the face above past two bolts to the top. Pro: To 3.5 inches.

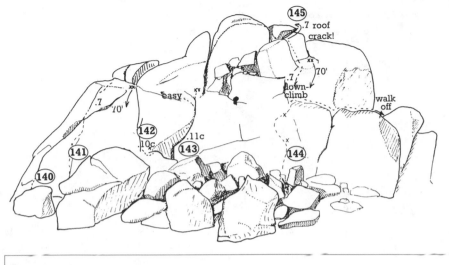

THE OLD WOMAN – EAST FACE

This is the first formation on the left (west) as you enter the campground. See map, page 36.

140 **Toe Jam (7) ★** Pro: To 2.5 inches.

141 **Judas (10b) ★** Pro: To 2.5 inches, two bolts.

142 **Bearded Cabbage (10c) ★★** Pro: To 3 inches, one bolt.

143 **Spider Line (11c) ★★★** Can be easily top-roped by climbing Bearded Cabbage and traversing over to bolts. Pro: Thin to 2.5 inches.

144 **Deviate (10a/b)** Make a funky mantle move past a bolt. Pro: To 2.5 inches.

145 **Geronimo (7) ★** A classic finish to the not so classic Deviate. Pro: To 3 inches.

THE OLD WOMAN – WEST FACE

146 **Dogleg (8) ★★** Descend off back side, from Deviate rappel. Pro: To 2.5 inches.

147 **Double Cross (7+) ★★★** Classic jamming exercise. Rap from top. Pro: To 3 inches.

148 **Band Saw (10c) ★** Kinda wild face climbing. Descend off back from Bearded Cabbage rappel. Pro: To 2 inches, three bolts.

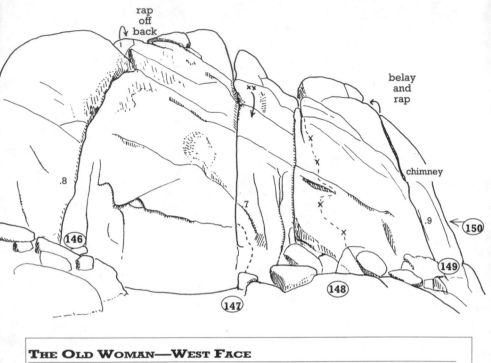

THE OLD WOMAN—WEST FACE

146 *Dogleg (8)* ★★	149 *Orphan (9+)* ★★
147 *Double Cross (7+)* ★★★	150 *Dandelion (9/10a)* ★
148 *Band Saw (10c)* ★	

149   **Orphan (9+)** ★★   Stemming and jamming lead to chimney. Descend Bearded Cabbage rappel. Pro: To 3+ inches.

150   **Dandelion (10a)** ★   Located on the south end of the rock. Climb a right arching crack, then up a thin crack which leads to face climbing past one bolt. Descend Bearded Cabbage rappel Pro: To 2 inches.

THE BLOB

This aptly-named formation lies on the left (west) side of the campground, near its north end. See map, page 36.

EAST FACE

151   **Buissonier (7)** ★   Climb the right-facing corner. Pro: Thin to 2 inches.

152   **Papa Woolsey (10b)** ★★   The original sport-type face climb, and still popular. Pro: Five bolts, medium pro for anchors.

153   **Mama Woolsey (10a R)** ★   A nice little climb, just sparse on the protection. Pro: Thin to 2 inches.

WEST FACE

154 **The Bong (4)** ★   Start in the small canyon up near the northern end of the rock. Climb the wide crack to face climbing. Pro: To 3 inches.

155 **Hoblett (7)**

156 **Beginner's Two (2)**   Pro: To 3 inches.

157 **Beginner's One (3)**   Pro: To 3 inches.

158 **Hobbit Roof (10d)** ★   A classic short problem. Many people avoid the crux face climb at the bottom and just climb the fun (10b) roof crack. Easily toproped or led. Pro: To 2 inches.

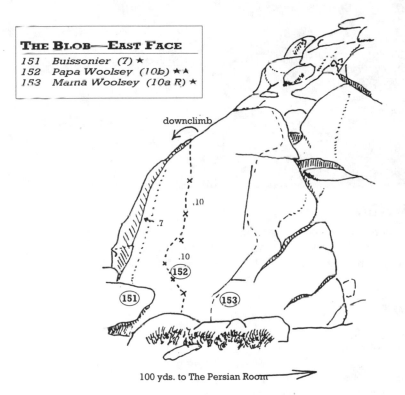

THE BLOB—EAST FACE

151   Buissonier (7) ★
152   Papa Woolsey (10b) ★★
153   Mama Woolsey (10a R) ★

downclimb

.10

.7

.10

(152)

(151)

(153)

100 yds. to The Persian Room

THE BLOB— WEST FACE
154   The Bong (4) ★
155   Hoblett (7)
156   Beginner's Two (2)
157   Beginner's One (3)
158   Hobbit Roof (10d) ★

THE WALL

This formation is very long, somewhat discontinuous. It is located directly east of both the Blob and The Old Woman. Its north end starts just south of Outhouse Rock and extends south to a point just east of Chimney Rock. See map, page 36.

THE WALL—NORTH END

Directly east of the vertical east face of The Blob, near the northeast end of the campground (just right of the apex of the campground loop) lies the northern end of a long rock ridge termed: The Wall. The northern end of The Wall has three boulders lying on its summit, the right-hand boulder being the largest. A straight-in crack on the right, which begins in a small corner is Hands Off (5.8). The descent is a walk off to the left. See map, page 36.

159   **Two Scoops Please   (10c R)** ★   Start up the initial crack of Hands Off, but then head up and left on face climbing. Pro: Two bolts, nuts for anchor.

160   **Hands Off** (8) ★★   This route climbs the obvious straight-in crack
  .   mentioned above, and ends on a ledge below the large boulders.
       Pro: Thin to 2 inches.

THE WALL – SOUTH END

*The southern end of The Wall lies about 40 yards northeast of Chimney Rock
and faces west toward the campground. It is due east and easily seen from
the Campground Bulletin Board. It is characterized as a smooth face split by a
chimney-crack system. The following climbs lie on the section of face just
right of the chimney system. From the vicinity of the Bulletin Board, the face
lies to the right and behind Chimney Rock. See map, page 36.*

161   **Chalk Up Another One** (10a) ★★   Start 25 feet right of the
       obvious chimney in the middle of the formation. Face climb past
       two bolts up into a bowl and then move left. Continue up past two
       more bolts to easier ground, a fifth bolt protects entry to a flared
       crack leading to the top. Pro: To 2.5 inches, five bolts.

162   **Pumping Ego** (10b) ★   Start about 12 feet right of Chalk Up
       Another One (35 feet right of the obvious chimney). Climb up past
       two bolts then head up and right past some horizontal breaks and
       two more bolts. Pro: Four bolts, nuts for anchor.

CHIMNEY ROCK – WEST FACE

*This rock is located at the east side of the campground, just east of where the
dirt road to Echo Cove and Barker Dam heads off the paved loop road (at the
Bulletin Board). From the Bulletin Board, it lies straight east about 150 yards
away. See map, page 36.*

163   **Loose Lips** (11a) ★★   The entire block froming the traversing
       crack has fallen off. Not climbable.

164   **West Face Overhang** (7) ★   A nice and varied easy route. Pro:
       To 3 inches.

165   **Fear of Flying** (10d R)   A little loose. Pro: Several small cams to
       2.5 inches, two bolts.

166   **Howard's Horror** (7) ★   (Direct 10b, R) Pro: To 2.5 inches.

167   **Break Dancing** (11a)   Pro: To 2 inches, three bolts.

168   **Damper** (9) ★   A nice wide crack (if that isn't an oxymoron). Pro:
       To 4 inches.

169   **Pinched Rib** (10b) ★★   This route is a perennial Joshua favorite.
       Originally rated 5.7, several large holds on the dike have cut loose
       over the years! Pro: Two bolts, nuts for belay.

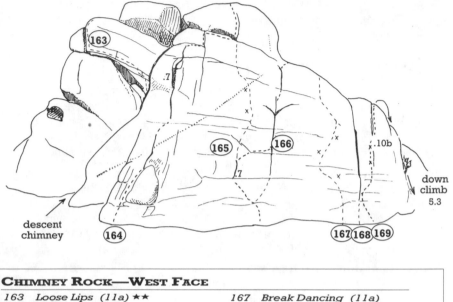

CHIMNEY ROCK—WEST FACE

163 *Loose Lips (11a)* ★★	167 *Break Dancing (11a)*
164 *West Face Overhang (7)* ★	168 *Damper (9)* ★
165 *Fear of Flying (10d R)*	169 *Pinched Rib (10b)* ★★
166 *Howard's Horror (7)* ★	

CHIMNEY ROCK – EAST FACE

170   The Flue (8) ★   This route lies left of the middle of the east side of Chimney Rock. Face climb up horizontals to reach an obvious right-diagonalling crack system that ends in a cave. Descend down the gully chimney on the west face. Pro: To 3 inches.

CYCLOPS ROCK

This formation lies outside Hidden Valley Campground, about 300 yards east of the entrance. See map, page 36.

NORTHEAST FACE

171   Overnight Sensation (11b) ★   This route lies on the northeast face of the formation. Climb face and cracks starting below and left from a brown, scooped-out "roof" that resembles a Volkswagen bug. Pro: Three or four bolts, small to 2 inches.

NORTHWEST FACE

This is the side of the formation that faces Hidden Valley Campground and is characterized by a deep chimney system in the center of the face (The Eye).

CYCLOPS ROCK—WEST FACE

172	Surface Tension (10d) ★★	175	Leader's Fright (8 R) ★★
173	The Eye (3 R) ★★	176	Dyna Damage (11b/c) ★
174	Telegram For Mongo (10c R) ★	177	Grey Cell Green (11b) ★★

172 **Surface Tension (10d) ★★** This route starts about 20 feet left of the deep chimney of The Eye by jumping up to a "hole." Four bolts protect face climbing up and left. Scary to the first bolt. Pro: Four bolts, nuts to 2.5 inches (anchors).

173 **The Eye (3 R) ★★** This route ascends the back right side of the large central recess/chimney on the Northwest Face. The route tops out at The Eye, a hole through the top of the formation. Pro: To 3 inches.

174 **Telegram For Mongo (10c R) ★** This route starts to the left of the following climb. Class 3 scrambling up a steep gully (5.0), 70 feet right of the start of The Eye to a large ledge. Climb the dark face directly above the ledge past two bolts, then eventually traverse right on cracks to reach the top. Pro: Two bolts, cams to 2.5 inches.

175 **Leader's Fright (8 R) ★★** This climb starts to the right of the previous route, off the right end of the ledge system. Climb a crack which is tricky to protect and takes you to the summit.   Pro: To 2 inches.

176 **Dyna Damage (11b/c) ★** Start off the right end of the ledge where the two previous climbs begin. Pro: Five bolts, medium cams.

177   **Grey Cell Green (11b)** ★★   This 50 foot sport route lies on the west side of the rock, about 75 feet right and below the ledge were Telegram For Mongo and Leader's Fright begin. Start in a small cleft/corner, and climb up and left on steep rock past three bolts and one fixed pin to a two bolt anchor/rap.

THE OUTBACK

This area covers territory starting northwest of Hidden Valley Campground and continuing east in an arc to just west of the Echo Rock/Echo Cove area. See map, page36.

STEVE CANYON

This group of rocks lies 200 yards northwest of the gap between The Old Woman and the Blob. They can be approached easily from either the campground or from pullouts along Quail Springs Road located about a quarter-mile northwest of the campground. The formations form a canyon that runs in a north/south direction. Routes lie both within the canyon as well as on the east and west faces outside the canyon. See map, page36.

UPPER WEST SIDE (East Face)

The west side of Steve Canyon is broken into two parts. The upper formation is distinguished by large roofs located about halfway up.

178   **Let's Get Horizontal (11b TR)** ★   Start about five feet left of Super Roof. Climb past horizontals. Pro: Gear and slings needed for anchor.

179   **Super Roof (9)** ★★   This is the left-hand crack splitting the roof. Pro: To 3 inches.

UPPER EAST WALL (West Face)

This formation lies on the upper right side of Steve Canyon, about 100 feet left of the Lower East Wall. The main face is characterized by a large chimney which splits it into two distinct sections. Several face and crack climbs lie on these faces. Descend down under a wedged block to the left.

180   **Grain Surgery (10a/b)** ★★   This route lies on the left side of the face that is left of the chimney mentioned above. Start up the shallow crack near the central part of the face, head up and left on horizontals to open face climbing past two bolts. Pro: Several cams to 2 inches, two bolts.

181   **Deflowered (6)** ★   This good, easy route lies about ten feet right of the large central chimney system. The route begins as a wide crack-chimney and becomes a hand crack above.   Pro: To 3 inches.

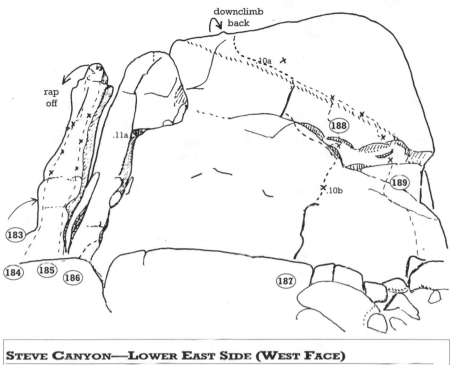

STEVE CANYON—LOWER EAST SIDE (WEST FACE)

183	Skinny Dip (7 R) ★	
184	Invisible Touch (10d) ★	
185	King Pin (11a/b R) ★	
186	Jumping Jack Crack (11a) ★★	

187	Sidewinder (10b) ★★★.	
188	Diamondback (10b/c) ★★	
189	Kingsnake (12b) ★	

182 **The Decompensator of Lhasa (10d) ★★** A high-angle smearing classic. Climb a thin left-arching crack to the left of Deflowered, then up horizontals to bolt protected face climbing. At the third bolt traverse right onto the arête past one more bolt to the top. Pro: Several .5 to 2 inches, four bolts.

LOWER EAST SIDE (West Face)

183 **Skinny Dip (7 R) ★** Follow a hand crack to a tunnel-through, then go up the chimney to the top.

184 **Invisible Touch (10d) ★** The three-bolt route just right of Skinny Dip, leads to a crack. Pro: Three bolts, thin to 2 inches. two-bolt anchor/rap on summit.

185 **King Pin (11a/b R) ★** Another three-bolt face route on the right side of the west face of the pillar; just left of an arête. Pro: Three bolts, two-bolt anchor/rap.

186   **Jumping Jack Crack (11a)** ★★   Climb the chimney until hard moves up into a thin crack (crux) lead to more cracks to the top. Pro: To 2 inches.

187   **Sidewinder (10b)** ★★★   A Joshua favorite. A little scary on the traverse, but the moves are not really very hard. Hardest move is going past first bolt. Pro: Medium to 2.5 inches.

188   **Diamondback (10b/c)** ★★   Not as difficult as it looks and a great variation to Sidewinder. Pro: Gear to 2 inches for anchor.

189   **Kingsnake (12b)** ★   A very difficult thin crimping problem over a ceiling. Join the previous routes to finish. Pro: For anchor.

PATAGONIA PILE

Patagonia Pile is approximately 450 yards north/northwest of the apex of the Hidden Valley Campground loop. A trail leads from the deep campsite just east of The Blob (containing a large, squarish boulder) out to an open area, then to the north of the campground. Patagonia Pile is the square-looking formation with an overhanging east face. See map, page 36.

190   **Wet Rock Day (11a/b TR)**

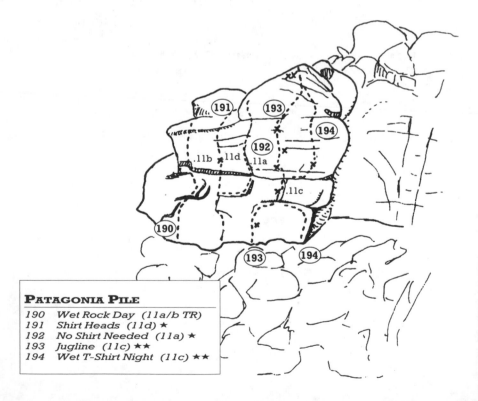

PATAGONIA PILE	
190	*Wet Rock Day (11a/b TR)*
191	*Shirt Heads (11d)* ★
192	*No Shirt Needed (11a)* ★
193	*Jugline (11c)* ★★
194	*Wet T-Shirt Night (11c)* ★★

191 **Shirt Heads (11d)** ★   Pro: Thin to 2 inches, one bolt.

192 **No Shirt Needed (11a)** ★   Start same as Shirt Heads, but head out right and follow a thin crack over a roof. Pro: Several thin to 2 inches.

193 **Jugline (11c)** ★★   Pro: Thin to 2 inches, five bolts.

194 **Wet T-Shirt Night (11c R)** ★★   The original line on the rock. Start to the right and traverse left to join Jugline. Pro: Thin to 2 inches, two bolts.

ROCK HUDSON

Rock Hudson is located about 150 yards north of Outhouse Rock. For routes 196-198, walk off right. See map, page 36.

195 **Absolute Zero (10c)** ★   Pro: Three bolts, nuts for anchor. Downclimb left.

196 **Looney Tunes (9)** ★   Pro: To 3 inches.

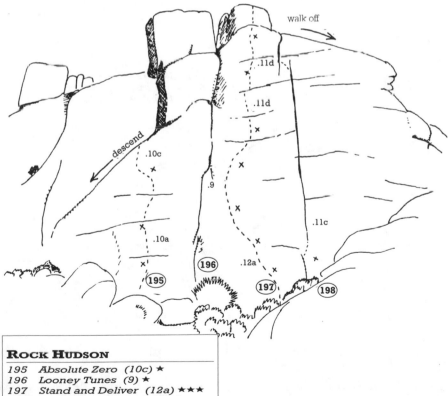

ROCK HUDSON		
195	*Absolute Zero (10c)* ★	
196	*Looney Tunes (9)* ★	
197	*Stand and Deliver (12a)* ★★★	
198	*Hot Rocks (11c)* ★★★194	

197   **Stand and Deliver (12a) ★★★**   A excellent thin face climb. Pro: Eight bolts, .5 to 1.5-inch camming units for horizontals.

198   **Hot Rocks (11c) ★★★**   One of the classic cracks of Joshua. Many people toprope this route, but other than the entry moves, the route is well protected. Pro: Several thin to 3 inches.

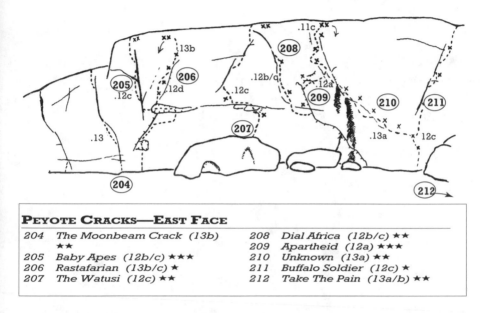

PEYOTE CRACKS—EAST FACE

204	The Moonbeam Crack (13b) ★★	208	Dial Africa (12b/c) ★★
205	Baby Apes (12b/c) ★★★	209	Apartheid (12a) ★★★
206	Rastafarian (13b/c) ★	210	Unknown (13a) ★★
207	The Watusi (12c) ★★	211	Buffalo Soldier (12c) ★
		212	Take The Pain (13a/b) ★★

THE PEYOTE CRACKS

This small but often climbed formation is about 250 yards northeast of Rock Hudson; roughly between Hidden Valley Campground and Echo Cove. Its west face is less vertical and has three prominent cracks. The east face is overhanging and contains a number of excellent and difficult routes. The formation is an easy walk from Hidden Valley Campground. A small parking area near Echo Cove Rocks also provides good access. See map, page 36.

WEST FACE

The west face has three obvious cracks (Left, Middle and Right Peyote Cracks).

199   **Left Peyote Crack (10c/d) ★**   This is the left-most of the three cracks. Pro: To 2 inches.

200   **Middle Peyote Crack (9+) ★**   The middle crack, gets wider up higher. Pro: To 2 inches.

201   **Right Peyote Crack (8) ★**   The right crack. Pro: To 2.5 inches.

202   **Face It (10a R/X)** ★   A one bolt face route 15 feet right of the
Right Peyote Crack.

203   **When You're A Poodle (11b R)** ★   A two-bolt climb around and
right of Face It.

EAST FACE (aka BACHAR toprope WALL)

*This overhanging face contains many difficult and excellent routes. Many of
these routes were toprope problems that have since been led; in some cases,
bolts have been added to protect these leads. Most of these routes are good
sport climbs. See map, page36.*

204   **The Moonbeam Crack (13b)** ★★   This route has been led, but
most prefer a toprope. Pro: From .25 to 2 inches.

205   **Baby Apes (12b/c)** ★★★   Pro: Thin to 2 inches. Most will
toprope.

206   **Rastafarian (13b/c)** ★   Pro: Thin to 2 inches, four bolts.

207   **The Watusi (12c)** ★★   Pro: To 2 inches, three bolts.

208   **Dial Africa (12b/c)** ★★   Pro: Very thin to 2 inches, four bolts
(poorly located).

209   **Apartheid (12a)** ★★★   Pro: Four bolts, 1.5 inch cam optional.

210   **Unknown (13a)** ★★   Start at Buffalo Soldier, clip the second bolt
and head left past more bolts, eventually joining Apartheid.
Pro:Nine bolts.

211   **Buffalo Soldier (12c)** ★   A very bouldery start leads to easier and
undistinguished climbing. Pro: To 2 inches, four bolts.

212   **Take The Pain (13a/b)** ★★   This four-bolt route lies on a separate
face about 70 feet right of Buffalo Soldier. Stick clip the first bolt.

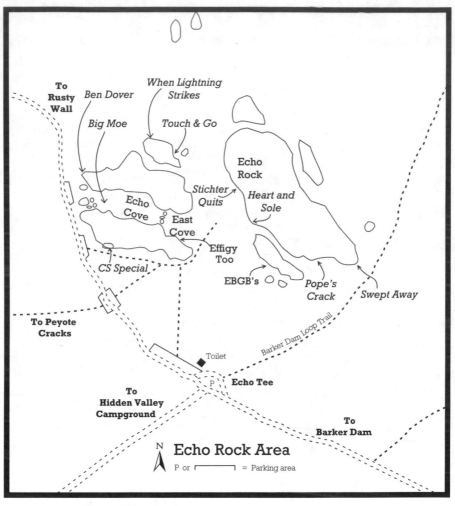

Echo Rock Area

P or ▭ = Parking area

ECHO ROCK AREA

This area lies about .7 mile to the northeast of Hidden Valley Campground. The dirt road leading to Echo Rock begins just south of Chimney Rock. A large parking area marks the spot where the road "tees" (Echo Tee). The road is called Big Horn Pass Road. The road to the northwest leads to Keys Ranch, an old ranch site that is off limits to all but guided tours. If you head right (east) from Echo Tee, you'll pass parking areas for the Comic Book Area, Barker Dam and Wonderland of Rocks, and eventually get back to the main, paved park road (Queen Valley Road).

RUSTY WALL

From Echo Cove (.25 mile north of Echo Tee), follow the dirt road (may be closed) for about .75 mile to a gate/fence for Keys Ranch. A short hike west (of about 400 yards) leads to the base of this orange-tinted, overhanging wall. Two cracks are located on the wall. (See map, page 52.)

213 Wangerbanger (11c) ★★★ This is the left thin-hands crack. Pro: Several to 2.5 inches.

214 O'Kelley's Crack (10c/d) ★★★ This is the right crack and on many climbers' top ten lists. The start is 5.11 and can be done several ways (e.g.: fist jam, lieback or face climb from the right). Pro: To 4 inches.

215 Riddles In The Dark (11c TR) ★★ Climbs the shallow right-facing corner just right of O'Kelly's Crack.

216 Finish What You Started (11c/d) ★★ Starts the same as Riddles in The Dark, but heads up and right on a steep face past three bolts.

ECHO COVE

This little "cove" lies about .25 mile northwest of Echo Tee, on the right (east) side of the road. Routes are described in sequence as they lie on either wall of the cove. Right and left is used in reference to how you would view the walls if you were facing east into the cove. See map, page 52.

LEFT (north) SIDE

217 Ben Dover (10b/c) This route lies 80 feet left of Fun Stuff on a steep north-facing wall. Pro: Three bolts, two bolt anchor/rap.

218 Fun Stuff (8) ★ There is a variation that starts to the left with an additional bolt. Pro: One bolt, gear to 2 inches, two-bolt anchor/rap.

219 The Sound of One Shoe Tapping (8) ★ Pro: Three bolts, two bolt anchor/rap.

220 W.A.C. (8 R) ★ Pro: Two bolts, two-bolt anchor/rap.

221 Pepasan (9+) Pro: Three bolts.

222 Battle of Britain (10b) ★ Pro: Four bolts, gear for anchors. Downclimb gully.

223 R.A.F (9) ★ Pro: Two bolts, gear for anchor. Downclimb gully.

224 Pinky Lee (10d R) ★ Most people toprope it. Pro: Several thin to 2 inches.

ECHO COVE—LEFT (NORTH) SIDE

217	Ben Dover (10b/c)		221	Pepasan (9+)
218	Fun Stuff (8) ★		222	Battle of Britain (10b) ★
219	The Sound of One Shoe		223	R.A.F (9) ★
	Tapping (8) ★		224	Pinky Lee (10d R) ★
220	W.A.C (8 R) ★			

RIGHT (South) SIDE

The following routes lie on the steep right-hand end of the south (right) side of Echo Cove, almost directly opposite Fun Stuff/W.A.C. See map, page 52.

225 **Out For Lunch (11a)** ★ This route starts 40 feet right of Big Moe, at the black streak near the right end of the wall. Climb up and past a bolt to reach a horizontal crack, from here two variations (each with two bolts) are possible. One goes slightly left then straight up (11a), the other traverses farther left then up (10d). Pro: Medium to 3 inches, no fixed anchors.

226 **Big Moe (11a/b R/X)** ★★★ This route lies on the steep face between two large oak bush/trees. A difficult move above a scoop, leads past two horizontal cracks and a fun finish. Usually toproped (bolts on top).

227 **Boulder Dash (9)** ★ Start just left of Big Moe, and traverse up and left on big holds to the base of a dihedral which is climbed to the top. Direct starts are also possible. Pro: To 2.5 inches.

228 **Moe Town (12a)** ★   This climb starts about 60 feet left of Big Moe. Climb past a bolt to a ledge, then up past two more bolts (crux) to a horizontal crack (gear here). Head up and right past one more bolt to a bolt anchor.

229 **Deceptive Corner (7)** ★   This climb begins about 70 feet left of Big Moe, at the right end of a rocky ledge. Climb up and left on a diagonal crack to a large ledge. Above, climb a short corner to the top. Often done in two short pitches. Pro: To 2.5 inches.

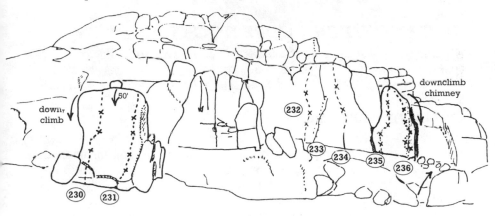

ECHO COVE ROCKS—SOUTH FACE

230 *R.M.L. (8)* ★	234 *Flake and Bake (8/9)* ★
231 *C.S. Special (10b)* ★★	235 *Sitting Here In Limbo (9)* ★
232 *Possessed By Elvis (10c)* ★	236 *Out On A Limb (10b/c)* ★★
233 *Bacon Flake (8/9)* ★	

SOUTH FACE

The Echo Cove Rocks form the cove itself, and the outer faces of these rocks contain many fine routes. The south face faces the road and lies adjacent to a fenced parking area. See map, page 52.

230 **R.M.L. (8)** ★   Go over a small roof, then past three bolts. Descend left or rap from anchor.

231 **C.S. Special (10b)** ★★   Four bolts near the right side of the large block. The start may be quite hard for shorter people. Pro: Four bolts. Descend left or rap.

232 **Possessed By Elvis (10c)** ★   Pro: One fixed pin, three bolts, gear to 2 inches. Descend right.

233 **Bacon Flake (8/9)** ★   The obvious crack in center of face. Pro: To 2.5 inches. Descend right.

234   **Flake and Bake (8/9) ★**   Start ten feet right of Bacon Flake in a
       thin crack, face climbing above. Pro: Thin to 2 inches, two bolts.
       Descend right.

235   **Sitting Here In Limbo (9) ★**   Pro: Five bolts, nuts for anchor.
       Descend the chimney behind.

236   **Out On A Limb (10b/c) ★★**   The start may be considerably
       more difficult if you're under 5'11" or so. Pro: Five bolts, gear for
       anchors. Descend the chimney behind.

EAST COVE/ECHO COVE ROCKS

*This small cove actually is a continuation of Echo Cove itself; a pile of
boulders separates the two areas. A trail connects the two. It lies about 75
yards farther right (east) from C.S. Special, just around the corner from Out
On A Limb. See map, page 52.*

EAST COVE – LEFT SIDE

*The east side of this small "cove" of rock is steep brown rock. Near the right
side of the face a hand crack starts about 15 feet off the ground; this crack is
Effigy Too. The easiest descent is down a chimney/gully directly behind the
face. The other side of the chimney is formed by the large boulder containing
Out On A Limb. You end up at the start of that route. See map, page 52.*

237   **The Real McCoy (12b TR) ★**   This route lies just right of the left-
       hand arête of the face, about 25 feet left of Halfway To Paradise.
       Start off a boulder, up a thin seam, then left and up a thin face to
       easier climbing above.

238   **Halfway To Paradise (10a R) ★★**   Start this route about 20 feet
       left of Effigy Too, climb up and left to a small sloping ledge,
       continue up past a bolt, then back right following easier climbing
       past many horizontal cracks. Pro: Many cams to 2 inches, one bolt.

239   **Effigy Too (10a/b) ★★**   Several difficult moves up and left give
       access to the bottom of the obvious hand crack near the right-hand
       end of the face. Pro: Thin to 2 inches.

240   **Misfits (11b) ★★**   Climb up the cracks and face past several bolts
       about 50 feet right of Effigy Too (on separate face). Pro: Small to 2
       inches, with several 1 to 1.5 inches.

EAST COVE – RIGHT SIDE

This wall directly faces Effigy Too et. al. (faces southwest). See map, page 52.

241   **Solo Dog (11b/c) ★★**   Near the right end of the face, face climb
       up a very thin crack to a horizontal break, then up past three bolts.
       Pro: Very thin to 1 inch, three bolts, two-bolt anchor/rap.

ECHO COVE FORMATIONS – EAST SIDE

An east-facing part of the Echo Cove Rock is about 110 yards to the right of Echo Cove, and roughly opposite the northwestern end of Echo Rock. The excellent-looking left facing corner is Touch and Go. See map, page 52.

242 **Touch and Go (9) ★★★** This is the fine left-facing corner mentioned above. To descend, head west and then downclimb into a rock filled gully/canyon to the left. Pro: To 2.5 inches.

243 **When Lightning Strikes (11c) ★★** This fine face climb lies about 150 feet right of Touch and Go, on the north face of a squarish block on the northern end of the main rock formations. Pro: Five bolts, nuts for anchors. Descend gap to the left.

ECHO ROCK

This rock lies nearly straight ahead (northeast) of the parking area at Echo Tee. The North (left) End is directly across from the east side of the Echo Cove formation. The South (right) End is best reached via an excellent trail (a continuation of an old road) that starts at the Echo Tee parking lot. This trail (the Barker Dam Loop Trail) also provides easy access to the Candy Bar Area. Climber trail markers have been placed to reduce the proliferation of "braided" trails through this area. Please reduce your impact on the desert by following these marked paths. Also, a toilet is located at the Echo Tee parking area. If you are climbing anywhere in the vicinity, please use this facility rather than leaving your waste in the desert.

NORTH END, WEST FACE

The west face of Echo Rock, due to its good rock and moderate angle, is ideally suited to face climbing. Theoretically, face climbs can be done almost anywhere, and the following list of routes clearly demonstrates this point. The addition of new bolted climbs only detracts from the existing routes. There are many excellent faces awaiting first ascents elsewhere in the park; new route attention should directed to those projects. Descend down slabs to the left. See map, page 52.

244 **Double Dip (6) ★★** Pro: Four to five bolts, optional gear to 2.5 inches.

245 **Battle of The Bulge (11c/d) ★** Aptly named route with a definite crux. Pro: Four bolts.

246 **Unzipper (10c R)** Runout. Pro: Two bolts.

247 **Try Again (10c R) ★** Pro: Three bolts.

248 **Minute Man (10d R)** Pro: Three bolts.

249 **Gone In 60 Seconds (10b/c R)** Crux is past first bolt. Pro: Four bolts.

250 **Cherry Bomb (10c R) ★** Pro: Three bolts.

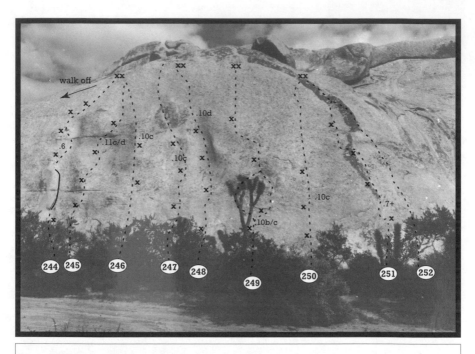

251   **Stichter Quits (7+)** ★★   An Echo classic and always popular. Pro: Four bolts.

252   **Dave's Solo (10a X)** Toprope it.

253   **Eye of The Storm (10a R)**   Pro: Three bolts.

254   **Legolas (10c)** ★   Pro: Thin nuts, three bolts.

255   **Stick To What (10a)** ★★   Pro: Four bolts.

256   **Forbidden Paradise (10b)** ★★★   A great, well-protected slab route. Pro: Six bolts.

257   **Ten Conversations at Once (10a)** ★   Pro: Cam to 4 inches, one bolt (no hanger).

258   **Fall From Grace (10b/c)** ★   Pro: Three bolts.

259   **April Fools (10c R)** Pro: Two bolts.

260   **Quick Draw McGraw (10b)**   Pro: Three bolts.

261   **The Falcon and The Snowman (10b/c R)** ★   Pro: Four bolts.

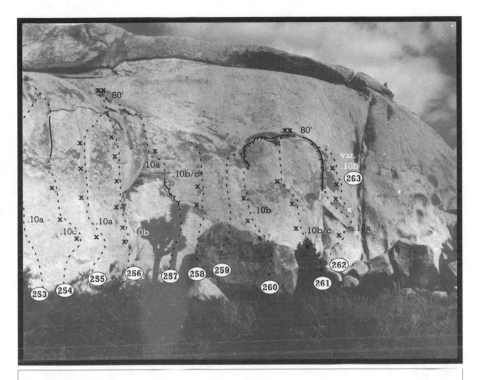

ECHO ROCK WEST FACE—RIGHT END

253	Eye of The Storm (10a R)	259	April Fools (10c R)
254	Legolas (10c) ★	260	Quick Draw McGraw (10b)
255	Stick To What (10a) ★★	261	The Falcon and The Snowman
256	Forbidden Paradise (10b) ★★★		(10b/c R) ★
257	Ten Conversations at Once	262	Heart and Sole (10a) ★★★
	(10a) ★	263	Love and Rockets (10b) ★
258	Fall From Grace (10b/c) ★		

262 **Heart and Sole (10a) ★★★**   An Echo classic; a little funky to first bolt. Pro: Three bolts, thin to 1.5 inches.

263 **Love and Rockets (10b) ★**   A variation to Heart and Sole. Pro: Four bolts.

264 **Highway 62 (9+ R) ★★**   A 250 foot long, rising girdle traverse of Echo Rock. Starts at first bolt of Double Dip, then goes up and right. From second bolt of Gone in 60 Seconds, go more or less straight right eventually reaching the second to last bolt on Forbidden Paradise. Follow Forbidden Paradise up to the top. Not a good choice on a crowded weekend.

EBGB AREA

A large block (the EBGB's Block) sits high on a pile of rocks to the right and west of the West Face of Echo Rock. A narrow corridor runs between the block and Echo Rock. The large block has several high-angled face routes on it. Descend off the block down a chimney on the back (east) side. See map, page 52.

265   **Jane's Getting Serious (12b/c)** ★★   This is a six-bolt climb 40 feet left of EBGB'S on the northwest face. A very difficult move over the overhang at the bottom (which can be aided, A0) leads to steep and excellent face climbing (11b).

266   **EBGB'S (10d)** ★★★   This route starts near the southwest corner of the EBGB's Block. A difficult move up, leads to an easy traverse out onto the west face; continue up to the top. Leader might consider pulling the rope through and dropping the end to better belay the second. Pro: Five bolts.

ECHO ROCK – SOUTH END

Descent from Pope's Crack, etc., is either by walking off to the left, down a gully/chimney and through boulders, or rappelling off the top of British Airways. Descent for Sole Fusion et al., is either Downclimb around by Sole Fusion or walk off over top of the formation to top of the West Face routes. See map, page 52.

267   **Pope's Crack (9)** ★★★   Downclimb left or rap from atop British Airways. Pro: To 2.5 inches.

268   **British Airways (11a R)** ★★   Pro: To 2 inches, two bolts, two-bolt anchor/rap.

269   **Rule Britannia (11c R)** ★★   Rap from British Airways. Pro: To 2 inches, four bolts.

270   **Raked Over The Coles (10d)** ★   Pro: Thin cams to 3 inches.

271   **Sole Fusion (12b/c)** ★★★   Pro: Three bolts, nuts for anchors.

272   **My Idea of Fun (12d)** ★   Pro: Six bolts. Rap from atop Swept Away.

273   **Street Sweeper (12a)** ★   Either continue up crux of Swept Away, or belay at end of Swept Away's first pitch and rap off. Pro: Three bolts, thin cams optional, plus gear for Swept Away.

274   **Swept Away (11a)** ★★★   Start at the base of the buttress, then traverse out left below roof. Pro: Thin to 1 inch, five bolts, fixed pin.

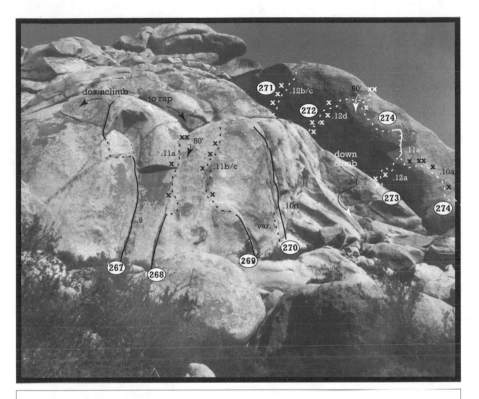

275   **T.S. Special (9 R)** ★   Start at the base of the buttress (same start as Swept Away), but go straight up the buttress over the roof (the scary/crux). Pro: Thin to 2 inches.

MORE FUNKY THAN MONKEY

This small formation lies about 200 yards west of the Barker Dam road and about 200 yards north of Big Horn Pass Road. The low formation is marked by a 20-foot roof about 30 feet off the ground. See map, page 66.

276   **More Monkey Than Funky (11c)** ★★   This route can be led (using two ropes), but is usually toproped. Pro: Several 1 to 3 inches. Bolts on top.

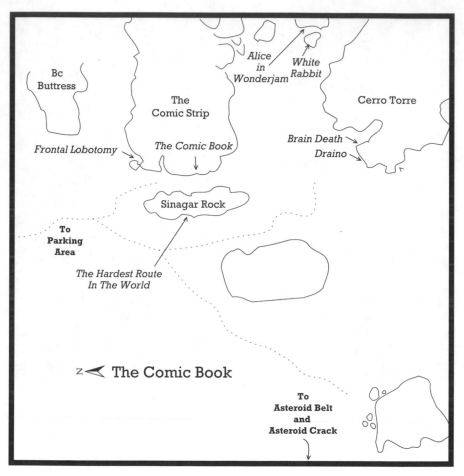

THE COMIC BOOK AREA

The Comic Book Area lies to the south of Big Horn Pass Road and is most easily approached from a point about 600 yards west of the Barker Dam turnoff. Two small parking areas on the south side of the road are located about 100 yards apart. The main Comic Book area is about .5 mile south of Big Horn Pass Road. The area consists of several distinct buttresses/ridges of rock against the hillside. The main formation containing Comic Book, (10a), is The Comic Strip; up and right from Comic Book is the Alice In Wonderland Area, and to the right (southwest) is Cerro Torre (named for the main tower's strong resemblance to . . . what else).

THE COMIC STRIP

The Comic Strip is the main formation/buttress of rock in the Comic Book area. The middle west face of the Comic Strip has an obvious crack leading to a "hole;" this is Comic Book (10a).

277 Frontal Lobotomy (10a) ★★ Most people avoid the first pitch and do the better second pitch. Either downclimb to the left or rap 100 or more feet from bolts (two ropes). Pro: Thin to 2 inches.

278 Full Frontal Nudity (10a) ★ This is a two-pitch climb. Start up the crack of Comic Book, traverse left on a dike to a belay. Somewhat runout face climbing past three bolts straight up to the top. Descend either right or left (easy class 5). Pro: To 4 inches, three bolts.

279 Comic Book (10a) ★★ This follows an obvious crack for two pitches. Belay in the "hole." Descend to the right. Pro: To 4 inches.

SINAGAR ROCK

Sinagar Rock is the formation that lies immediately west of the Comic Strip forming the small talus filled canyon below Comic Book. The following climb lies on the middle of the southwest face. See map page 62.

280   **The Hardest Route in the World (12c/d)** ★★   This is a six bolt route with good protection and hard moves. Some people break the climb into two pitches by belaying on a shelf at the second bolt. Pro: Six bolts, two fixed pins, two-bolt anchor.

ALICE IN WONDERLAND AREA

This is the jumble of large boulders and rocks up and right (southeast) of The Comic Strip. Two crack routes (Combination Locks and Alice in Wonderjam) lie on a brownish wall on the left, the two face climbs lie on a large boulder/slab to the right. See map page 62.

281   **Combination Locks (11c)** ★   Climb the thin left-hand crack. There is one bolt at the start. Pro: To 2 inches, one bolt.

282   **Alice in Wonderjam (9)** ★★   This is the right-hand fingers to fist crack. Pro: To 2.5 inches.

283   **White Rabbit (10a R)** ★   The left-hand slab route. Pro: Two bolts, nuts for anchor.

284   **Black Rabbit (9+)** ★   Climb the better protected face right of White Rabbit. Pro: Four bolts, nuts for anchor.

CERRO TORRE AREA

The Cerro Torre area is the complex of formations and buttresses down and to the right of the Alice In Wonderland Area and directly right (south) of The Comic Strip. There are three cracks on the right (west) side of a small box canyon. See locations of routes on map page 62.

285   **Brain Death (12a)** ★★   This is the right-hand of three distinct cracks on the right side of the canyon. Start off a small pinnacle/boulder to reach the thin crack which then jogs left. Pro: Thin to 1.5 inches.

286   **Brain Damage (12a R)** ★   Start right of Brain Death. Face climb past a bolt then head up and right to thin cracks. A long fall is a definite possibility. Pro: Thin to 1.5, one bolt.

287   **Draino (10b)** ★   This hand crack lies around the corner and to the right of the previous climbs (outside the box canyon) facing in a northerly direction. Pro: To 2.5 inches.

ALICE IN WONDERLAND AREA

281   Combination Locks (11c) ★   **Cerro Torre Area**
282   Alice in Wonderjam (9) ★★   285   Brain Death (12a) ★★
283   White Rabbit (10a R) ★   286   Brain Damage (12a R) ★
284   Black Rabbit (9+) ★   287   Draino (10b) ★

ASTEROID BELT

This small formation lies about .5 mile west of the main Comic Book area. It also is about .5 mile east of Cyclops Rock, in Hidden Valley Campground. It is probably easier to approach this formation/route directly from the Hidden Valley Campground from the vicinity of Cyclops Rock (unless you are already at The Comic Book Area). Much bouldering lies around and to the right of Asteroid Crack. See map, page 62.

288   **Asteroid Crack (12d) ★★**   This extremely thin and rather short crack lies on the west side of The Asteroid Belt. More famous than it deserves, merely because of the innumerable photos appearing in climbing books and magazines. Pro: Many very thin to .75 inch.

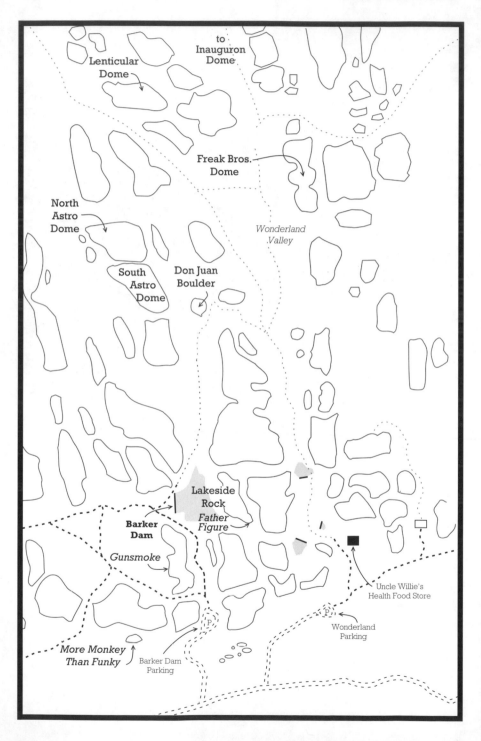

to
Inauguron
Dome

Lenticular
Dome

Freak Bros.
Dome

North
Astro
Dome

*Wonderland
Valley*

South
Astro
Dome

Don Juan
Boulder

Lakeside
Rock
*Father
Figure*

**Barker
Dam**

Gunsmoke

Uncle Willie's
Health Food Store

P

P

Wonderland
Parking

*More Monkey
Than Funky*

Barker Dam
Parking

BARKER DAM AREA

To reach Barker Dam from Echo Tee, turn right and follow the Big Horn Pass Road as it heads east. After about one mile, turn on a side road that heads north. This road ends after about 300 yards at a large parking area. A trail (which connects with the Barker Dam Loop Trail) heads straight north to Barker Dam, about 600 yards away.

GUNSMOKE BOULDERING AREA

To reach the Gunsmoke area from the Barker Dam parking area, head north for about 25 yards to a point where a trail heads west through some small boulders. This leads to a large, open basin extending to the west and north. The trail continues in a northwest direction and joins up with the Barker Dam Loop Trail. This excellent bouldering spot lies about 175 yards north of where the Barker Dam Loop Trail enters the open basin. Just as you enter the open basin, take an unmarked trail to the right that branches straight north. Because of the western facing aspect of this spot, it is popular on cool afternoons. See map, page 66.

289   **Gunsmoke (11+ V2)** ★★★   An excellent 75+ foot boulder traverse.

290   **High Noon (B1 V5 R)** ★★   Go straight up near the start of the Gunsmoke traverse on horizontals to reach a short thin crack and a rounded top. A very good spot, recommended.

291   **A Streetcar Named Desire (B1/2 V6)** ★★   This blank stemming corner is about 25 yards south of Gunsmoke just east of the approach trail (you pass it on the way to Gunsmoke) on the northwest side of boulder.

292   **The Tube (11- V0+)** ★★   Scary. This boulder problem lies about 50 yards northwest of Gunsmoke, on the western side of a large boulder (you can see the boulder from Gunsmoke). A thin crack/flake diagonals left, then funky face moves over a yucca put you on top.

LAKESIDE ROCK

Just as you get to Barker Dam, a large, low-angled dome can be seen to the right (east). This is Lakeside Rock. Map, page 66.

WEST FACE

293   **An Eye For an Eye and a Route For a Route (10b/c)** ★★   This slab climb lies near the middle of the low-angled west face of Lakeside rock. It is the right hand of the two central and long bolted face climbs. Pass a small roof/overhang at the bottom (the crux) then proceed past seven bolts on a good slab to a two-bolt anchor/rap. Pro: Seven bolts, small to med cams/nuts for roof at start.

EAST SIDE

The following routes are approached by walking right (south and then east) around the southern end of the formation. Look for some large blocky boulders and short, but steep, faces. See map page 66.

294   Patricide (11b) ★   This route climbs an arête on the right end of these steep faces. Pro: Two bolts/sport anchor.

295   Father Figure (13a) ★★★   This route is the left-hand route of two routes which lie on a southern facing and overhanging face to the right and around a large boulder from the previous climb. A popular "project" route with excellent moves and distinct crux. Pro: Four bolts, two-bolt anchor/rap.

296   Factor One (13b/c) ★★   This route lies on the rounded arête/face to the right of Father Figure. A little dicey getting to last bolt. Pro: Five bolts, two-bolt anchor/rap.

WONDERLAND OF ROCKS SOUTH

The southern part of the Wonderland of Rocks lies to the north and east of Barker Dam. Although you can also approach the southern Wonderland from Barker Dam, the most common (easiest) way to get into this area is from the Wonderland Ranch parking area and up the Wonderland Valley. Drive 200 yards, on the Big Horn Pass Road, past the Barker Dam turnoff; here, you'll find another turn off to the north. Follow this until it ends at a parking area. A bathroom (the only one in the area), and a trashcan are found here. Keep your impact to a minimum; use these facilities. From the parking area, head north to an old, burned-out building (Uncle Willie's Health Food Store). A wash to the left (west) of Uncle Willie's leads past a small dam to a valley that runs in a north-south direction. This is the southern end of the Wonderland Valley.

THE ASTRO DOMES

These two domes offer some of Joshua Tree's finest face climbing routes. The rock on the northeast faces of both the North and South Astro Domes is uncharacteristically smooth. Most routes climb sharp edges or flakes on excellent rock. The Astro Domes are about one mile up the wash from Uncle Willie's Health Food Store, just to the northwest from the point where the Wonderland Valley widens.

SOUTH ASTRO DOME – EASTERN SIDE

The easiest descent from South Astro Dome is down the northwest shoulder. This is Class 3. This means walking around the end of the North Astro Dome. Two single rope rappels (60 feet and 90 feet) or a single 140 foot rappel (two ropes), can be done from near the top of My Laundry. See topo, page 71.

297 **Hex Marks The Poot (7)** ★ This route lies on the extreme left end of the east face of the South Astro Dome, almost directly up from the huge Don Juan Boulder. It is the very obvious hands to offwidth crack. A second pitch can be added (8); climb up an obvious lieback flake. Pro: To 4 inches.

298 **Naked Singularity (11c)** ★ This route lies near the left side of the main face on more featured brownish rock. Climb up past three bolts to a flake, then head up and right to a bolt. Above climb over a small roof and then proceed past five more bolts to a two-bolt anchor. Make a 100+ foot rappel to the ground. Pro: Nine bolts, optional medium gear.

299 **Mamunia (13a)** ★★ This two pitch route follows a water streak up the very center of the bald face on the left portion of the South Astro Dome. It ends some 60 feet from the top. The first pitch is (12c). The second is (13a). Pro: Fourteen bolts, two raps from bolt anchors.

300 **Stone Idol (11d R)** ★★ An excellent, but bold venture. Pro: Six bolts, nuts for anchors

301 **My Laundry (9)** ★★ The first route on the east face of the Astro Domes. Pro: Thin to 1.5 inches, four bolts.

302 **Crimping Lessons (11c)** ★ If your tips are sore, better avoid this one. Pro: Five bolts, two-bolt anchor/rap.

303 **Solid Gold (10a)** ★★★ An all-time Joshua Tree classic outing and on many people's top ten lists. Both pitches are excellent. Gear is mandatory for belays. Pro: Thin to 1.5 inches, nine bolts.

304 **Middle Age Crazy (11b)** ★★ A little runout before joining Such A Savage. Pro: Seven bolts, medium nuts.

305 **Middle Age Savage (11d/12a)** ★★ Start about 50 feet right of Solid Gold (and right of Middle Age Crazy) and climb up past eight bolts to a two bolt anchor/rap. Shares crux and three bolts of Such A Savage. A sport route.

306 **Such A Savage (11a)** ★★★ A tremendous route. Start well to the right on slab moves that lead past two bolts, then traverse left to where the photo shows the rest of the route. The first pitch is a runout to the first and second bolts, but above is superb, steep, polished and very well protected face moves. The second pitch is

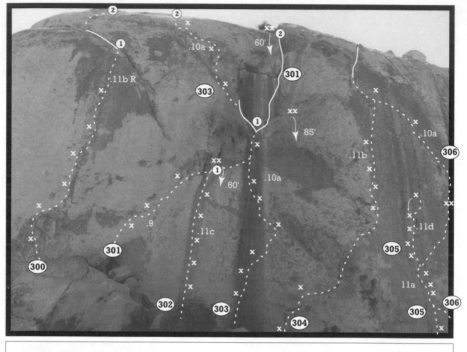

fantastic, though often ignored by myopic climbers. Pro: Eleven bolts, nuts to 1.5 inches.

307 **Breakfast of Champions (9 R)** ★   This route climbs the hand crack which starts just a short bit right of Such A Savage. (1) Climb the crack and flakes to a two-bolt belay in a "pod." (2) Somewhat run-out face climbing, up and right leads to the top. Not overly frightening. Pro: To 3 inches, one bolt.

308 **Piggle Pugg (10c)** ★   Climb a lieback flake to right of Breakfast of Champions and join that route. Pro: Many thin to 2 inches.

NORTH ASTRO DOME – NORTHEAST FACE

Several descents possible. Most popular is to make two 75+ foot rappels from near the summit (down and left) from rap anchors. You can also downclimb the northwest shoulder (4). Map, page 66.

309 **Repo Man (12a R)** ★★   An excellent though very dicey route, with the crux being runout and hard moves after that. Named after

original route was removed, then this first pitch was re-led and bolted. Pro: Four bolts, two-bolt anchor/rap.

310 **Figures on a Landscape (10b)** ★★★ Arguably the finest route in the park. Two or three pitches of excellent face and crack climbing that keeps your interest. Recommended for those comfortable at the grade. Pro: Eight bolts, nuts to 3 inches.

311 **The Gunslinger (12a)** ★★★ Perhaps the longest route in the park and certainly one of the better hard climbs. The bottom pitches are a bit flakey and need traffic. Many techniques needed and continuously difficult. Four pitches. Pro: Twenty-one bolts, nuts to 2.5 inches.

312 **Unknown Soldier (11b)** ★★ Another fine long route on the North Astro Dome. Pro: Nine Bolts, thin to 1.5 inches, and slings for flakes.

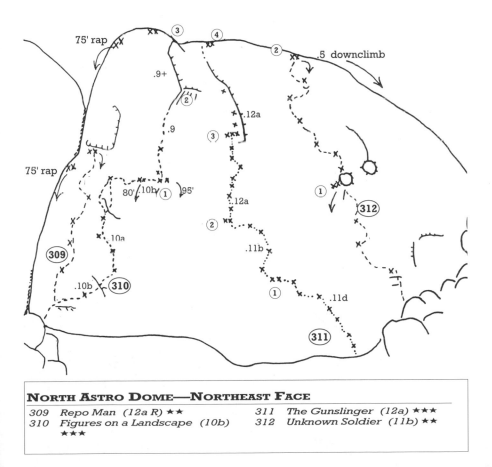

NORTH ASTRO DOME—NORTHEAST FACE

309 *Repo Man (12a R)* ★★	311 *The Gunslinger (12a)* ★★★
310 *Figures on a Landscape (10b)* ★★★	312 *Unknown Soldier (11b)* ★★

LENTICULAR DOME

This attractive rock lies about 450 yards north of the North Astro Dome. However, it is best approached via the main trail through the Wonderland Valley. Eventually, you must cut into a wash that heads northwest and passes directly below the southwest face of Lenticular Dome. The mottled face is characterized by a crack that ascends two-thirds up the face then stops (Mental Physics). A trail that heads north from near Don Juan Boulder leads directly into this wash and offers an alternative route. Descend to the left, then down slabs into a gully. See map, page66.

313   **Dazed and Confused (9+) ★★**   This is the bolted face climb that starts 20 feet left of Mental Physics. Can be done in one pitch (165+ foot rope needed), but is often broken into two pitches. Pro: bolts, bolt belay.

314   **Mental Physics (7+) ★★★**   Considered by most to be the best route of this grade in the park. This route climbs the obvious crack in the center of the southwest face to a belay. Continue up face climbing to the top. Pro: To 3 inches, one bolt.

FREAK BROTHERS DOMES—WEST FACE

315   I Can't Believe It's A Girdle (10a) ★★★
316   Girdle Crossing (10d) ★

FREAK BROTHERS DOMES – WEST FACE

This distinctive trio of domes is just north of Surprise Rock, and is recognizable by the three roofs that run through the domes. See map, page 66.

315   **I Can't Believe It's A Girdle (10a)** ★★★   R (for follower) A four pitch route that delivers lots of excitement. Pro: Fourteen bolts, nuts for some belays.

316   **Girdle Crossing (10d)** ★   Be careful of rope drag; you may not want to clip some traverse bolts or bring long slings. Pro: Eight bolts.

SECRET VALLEY

This canyon runs in a north-south direction, parallel to the Wonderland Valley but about 450 yards to the east. The best approach is to walk north in the Wonderland Valley from The Freak Brothers Dome for about 650 yards, then turn right into an east-west canyon that leads to Secret Valley. Several large west-facing rocks lie on the east side of Secret Valley. Inauguron Dome and Elephant Arches contain some excellent and longer routes that are more than worth the walk. Inauguron Dome is the right-hand (southern most) dome and Elephant Arches the northernmost dome. Not shown on the map.

INAUGURON DOME

The best descent is down 4th class slabs to the right of the main face, toward White Bread Fever. See photo.

317   **The Inauguron (11b/c)** ★★   The first pitch crux is a thin crack near the top. The second pitch is a good bolt protected face. Pro: Thin to 2 inches, bolts.

318   **Morality Test (11b R)** ★★   An excellent steep slab route. The best finish is the second pitch of Inauguron. Pro: To 2 inches, four bolts.

319   **Yardy-Hoo and Away (10a)** ★★   Perhaps a little runout in places, but an excellent adventure. Pro: Bolts, to 2 inches.

320   **White Bread Fever (11c)** ★★   This route lies on a higher, smaller face, about 75 yards to the right and up from the main face. This is the extreme right-hand climb. Face climb up past two bolts, then make a hard traverse up and left into a hand crack that continues up to a ledge. A short easy crack pitch leads to the top. Descend to the left then down the ramp, back right to the base. Pro: To 3 inches, two bolts.

INAUGURON DOME

317	The Inauguron (11b/c) ★★
318	Morality Test (11b R) ★★
319	Yardy-Hoo and Away (10a) ★★★194

ELEPHANT ARCHES

This formation lies about 100 yards directly to the north of Inauguron Dome in the same north-south canyon (Secret Valley). It faces west and is character-ized by a thin arch on its right slope. Descend easy Class 5 (5) down the right side, over the arch.

   321   **Vice President (10b/c R) ★★**   Start in the recess/crack 15 feet
          left of the following route. Above, the crack thins until it disappears
          completely. Place several pieces and you're now on runout face
          climbing (10b/c R) to the top. Pro: Thin to 3 inches.

322 **Black President (11a)** ★★★   This route follows discontinuous cracks and face climbing near the right-center section of the face. Face climb past a bolt into a shallow crack which leads to a thin face crux past a second bolt. Above, discontinuous cracks lead to the top. A must do route with lots of good and varied climbing. Pro: Thin to 2 inches, two bolts.

RYAN AREA

The remainder of this part of the guide covers crags as they are encountered along the Quail Springs Road. From Hidden Valley Campground, Quail Springs Road heads south for about two miles to a point where the Key's View Road branches off right. The Quail Springs Road curves east, then northeast, from here. From the point of its intersection with the Key's View Road, Quail Springs Road changes names (probably just to confuse people). For about the next eleven miles, the main road is now called Sheep Pass Road.

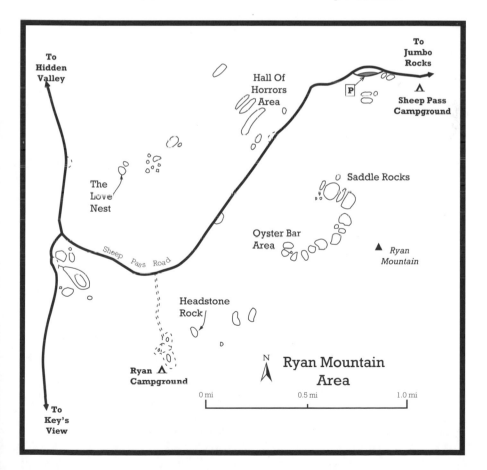

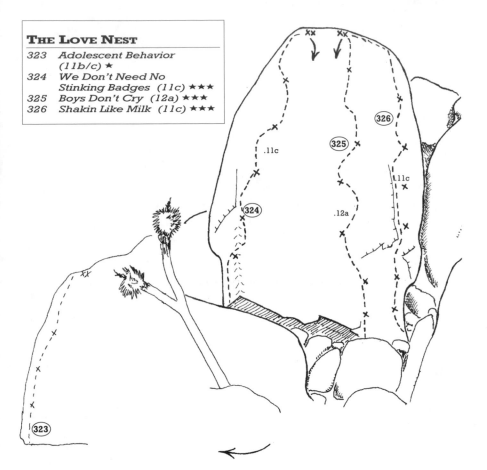

THE LOVE NEST

323   Adolescent Behavior
      (11b/c) ★
324   We Don't Need No
      Stinking Badges (11c) ★★★
325   Boys Don't Cry (12a) ★★★
326   Shakin Like Milk (11c) ★★★

THE LOVE NEST

This area lies about .3 miles east of the Quail Springs Road at a point 1.3 miles south of Hidden Valley Campground and a third of a mile before you get to the Cap Rock/Key's View Road turnoff. This is the first set of rocks encountered as you walk east from Quail Springs Road. The routes are located on the slightly-overhanging south face of the formation. Apparently, a large number of rattlesnakes spend the winter under The Love Nest formation. Care should be taken particularly in the Spring, when the snakes emerge. Do not disturb the snakes, they soon scatter throughout the park when temperatures warm.

    323   Adolescent Behavior (11b/c) ★   This route is located on the left (southwest) arête of a small rock just down and left (northwest) of The Love Nest formation. Pro: Three bolts.

    324   We Don't Need No Stinking Badges (11c) ★★★   Pro: Six bolts, bolt anchors.

325   **Boys Don't Cry (12a)** ★★★   Pro: Six bolts, bolt anchors.
326   **Shakin Like Milk (11c)** ★★★   Pro: Six bolts, bolt anchors.

RYAN CAMPGROUND

Ryan Campground is located about .75 mile east of Cap Rock, along the Sheep Pass Loop Road. Take a dirt road about .25 mile south to the actual campground. A few routes are located in the campground, while the balanced pillar to the east (Headstone Rock) provides the best and most popular routes. See map.

327   **Slightly Ahead of Our Time (12a)** ★   This is the bolt-ladder route on the large boulder in the west portion of the campground. It was also the first (12) route in Joshua Tree.

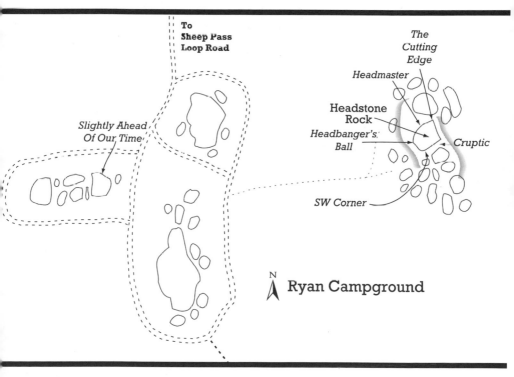

HEADSTONE ROCK

This pillar of rock sits on top of a jumble of rocks and boulders about 200 yards east of the campground. The first ascent of Headstone Rock was made in 1956 by Bob Boyle and Rod Smith. A rope, tossed over the summit, was climbed to reach the top. A single rope is sufficient for the rappel descent.

SOUTH FACE

328   **SW Corner (6)** ★★★   Start left of center of the south face, climb
       up and left to the arête, then to the top. One of Joshua's first routes
       and perhaps the best (if not most popular) route of this grade in the
       park. Pro: Four bolts.

329   **South Face Center (9 TR)** ★   Toprope the right-center of the
       face.

330   **Cryptic (8)** ★★   Climb the face just left of the southeast arête past
       three bolts.

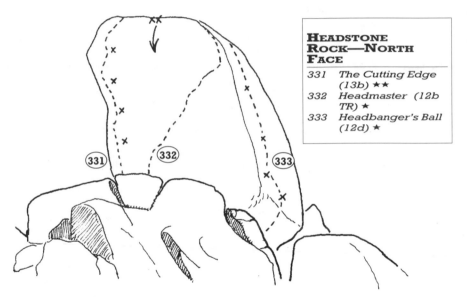

HEADSTONE
ROCK—NORTH
FACE

*331   The Cutting Edge
        (13b) ★★*
*332   Headmaster (12b
        TR) ★*
*333   Headbanger's Ball
        (12d) ★*

NORTH FACE

331   **The Cutting Edge (13b)** ★★   This route climbs the northeast
       arête of Headstone Rock. Pro: Four bolts (some hard to clip).

332   **Headmaster (12b TR)** ★   Start in the middle of the north face,
       climb up and right eventually reaching the right-hand arête below
       the top.

333   **Headbanger's Ball (12d)** ★   Start just right of the northwest arête,
       on the west face, climb more or less straight up. Pro: Four bolts.

OYSTER BAR AREA

*This area essentially is the lowest portion of the Cowboy Crags, a band of
cliffs that starts up and right (south) of Saddle Rocks and arches down the
hillside to the south. Park at a large turnout on the east side of the road about
.5 mile south of the Hall of Horrors and Saddle Rocks parking area. The
approach is a fairly level hike of about .3 mile. See map.*

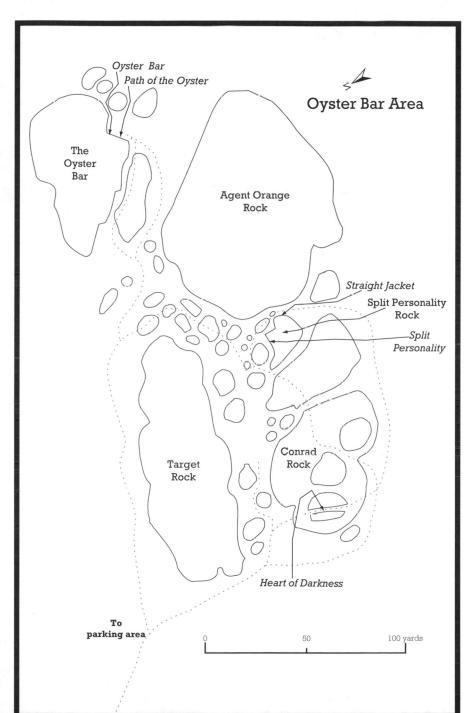

Oyster Bar
Path of the Oyster

Oyster Bar Area

The
Oyster
Bar

Agent Orange
Rock

Straight Jacket

Split Personality
Rock

Split
Personality

Target
Rock

Conrad
Rock

Heart of Darkness

To
parking area

0   50   100 yards

CONRAD ROCK

This formation is the southwestern-most formation, the right hand of the two formations closest to the road. Conrad Rock forms the southern part of the canyon between these two formations. A large split rock/boulder lies near the western end of Conrad Rock. Heart of Darkness lies in the narrow (north-south) corridor formed by this split rock. See map, page 79.

334 Heart of Darkness (11a) ★★★   This is the excellent thin crack on the west side of the narrow corridor. Pro: Many thin to 1.5 inches.

SPLIT PERSONALITY ROCK

This is really a large boulder that sits atop the eastern end of Conrad Rock. It is distinguished by a flat, vertical face that faces to the northwest. It can be seen from the road and can be approached several different ways. The usual approach is to go around the east end of the formation just north of Conrad Rock (Target Rock), then scramble up boulders to the base. See map, page 79.

335 Split Personality (11d) ★★★   This route climbs past five bolts on the arête of the vertical northwest face.

336 Disposition Crevice (11b) ★   Climb the dihedral around and left of Split Personality. Pro: Thin nuts and a bolt.

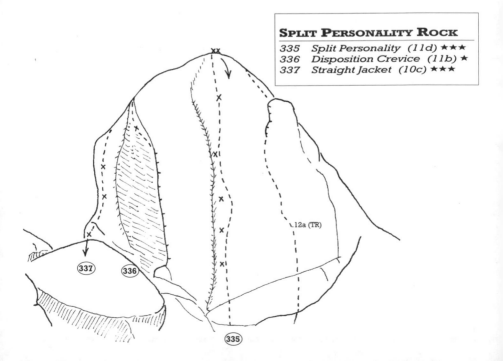

SPLIT PERSONALITY ROCK

335 *Split Personality (11d) ★★★*
336 *Disposition Crevice (11b) ★*
337 *Straight Jacket (10c) ★★★*

.12a (TR)

337   **Straight Jacket (10c) ★★★**   Start down and around the corner
      (left) from Split Personality. Climb the overhanging face to a friction
      face above, passing three bolts.

THE OYSTER BAR

*This formation lies to the northeast of
Target Rock, Conrad Rock, etc. A wide
gully on the west side of the rock
separates it from these formations. Walk
up this gully, then head east (left) to get
to the steep face routes on the south side
of the formation. A link-up (start on The
Oyster Bar and finish on Path of the
Oyster) (11d/12a) is also possible. See
map, page 79.*

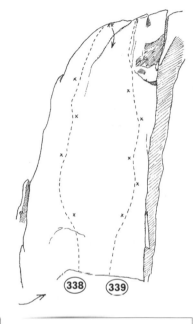

338   **Path of the Oyster (11c) ★★**
      This is the left-hand route on
      the south side of the formation.
      Pro: Four bolts, bolt anchor.

339   **The Oyster Bar (11a) ★★★**
      This is the five-bolt route on the
      right.

SADDLE ROCKS

*This very large slab of rock lies about
one mile northeast of Ryan Campground,
on the side of Ryan Mountain, to the east
of Sheep Pass Road. A series of car
pullouts on the right and left sides of*

THE OYSTER BAR		
338	Path of the Oyster (11c) ★★	
339	The Oyster Bar (11a) ★★★	

*Sheep Pass Road (also the parking area for the Hall of Horrors) leave about a
.5 mile walk eastward to the rock. The Hall of Horrors is on the west side of
the road. Please follow the climber trail/markers to reduce impact in this area.
See map, pages 75, 82.*

NORTH FACE

The following routes lie on the northern and northwest part of the lower
summit of Saddle Rocks. Most of these routes end at almost the same place.
Descent for these routes is usually via a rappel down the northeast side of
the rock (at the top of Right On).

340   **Space Mountain (10b) ★★**   Start at a giant, left-facing open book
      on the northeast corner of the lower formation. This is just below
      the rappel route on the north end of the lower formation. Follow a

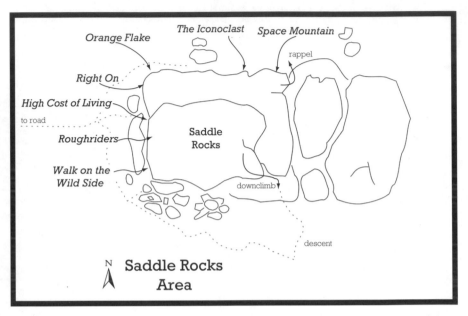

Orange Flake
The Iconoclast   Space Mountain
rappel
Right On
High Cost of Living
to road
Roughriders
Saddle
Rocks
Walk on the
Wild Side
downclimb
descent

N **Saddle Rocks**
      Area

traversing crack right until you can climb straight up the steep face above, past bolts. Pro: Thin (for start), all bolts above.

341 Raging Bull Dike (11d) ★★ This route starts about 50 feet left (and uphill) from The Iconoclast. Climb on a dike of sorts past four bolts to a small ledge with a two-bolt anchor/rap. An optional finish up a (8) crack above leads to the top of the rock. Pro: Four bolts (optional gear).

342 The Iconoclast (13a) ★★★ This route climbs the overhanging arête past eight bolts to a two-bolt anchor/rap. (see photo)

LOWER SUMMIT WEST FACE

These routes lie on the large, lower western slab of Saddle Rocks and are two to three pitches in length. Several descents are possible. Many people make two double rope rappels down Walk on The Wild Side (be careful if people are coming up that route). It is also possible to make two single rope rappels down the southwestern part of the rock, but some downclimbing is involved. Finally, you can head down the south side of the Lower Summit (downclimb a chimney), then either downclimb slabs below or rappel.

343 Orange Flake (8) ★ Start near a pine tree up the talus on the left side of the slab, several bolts heading straight up will be seen. (1) Climb to the first bolt (only), rather than continuing up, traverse right and slightly up past three more bolts until you reach the beginning of a long crack system. (2) Stay in this crack system for three more pitches reaching a notch. Make a 75 foot rappel down the back side. Walk off left. Pro: To 3 inches, four bolts.

SADDLE ROCKS

340   Space Mountain (10b) ★★
341   Raging Bull Dike (11d) ★★
342   The Iconoclast (13a) ★★★
Lower Summit West Face
343   Orange Flake (8) ★
344   Right On (5 R) ★★
345   Bosch Job (11d R) ★
346   The High Cost of Living (11a to
        12a depending on height) ★★

347   A Cheap Way to Die (10d) ★★
348   Roughriders (11b) ★★
349   Harlequin (10c R) ★★
350   Unknown (10c) ★
351   Dial 911 (10b) ★★
352   Walk On The Wild Side (8)
        ★★★
353   Negro Girls (9 R) ★

344   **Right On (5 R)** ★★   Start directly below the two long crack systems. Climb face past one bolt to reach the right hand crack/chimney. Follow this for three pitches, eventually heading left near the top to join the previous climb. Descend as on Orange Flake. Pro: To 3 inches, one bolt.

345   **Bosch Job (11d R)** ★   This is a bolted two-pitch climb between Right On and The High Cost of Living. Pro: Bolts, few nuts for bottom and top anchors.

346   **The High Cost of Living (11a to 12a depending on one's height)** ★★   Downclimb to the right. Pro: Bolts, few nuts for bottom and top anchors.

347   **A Cheap Way to Die (10d)** ★★   Walk, downclimb to the right. Pro: Bolts, few nuts for bottom and top anchors.

348   **Roughriders (11b)** ★★   Two pitches, then rap the route (two ropes). Pro: Fourteen bolts

349   **Harlequin (10c R)** ★★   Pro: Some thin to medium nuts, bolts.

350   **Unknown (10c)** ★   Rappel the next climb (two ropes needed). Pro: Lots of bolts.

351   **Dial 911 (10b)** ★★   Rap down the route (two ropes needed). Pro: Lots of bolts.

352   **Walk On The Wild Side (8)** ★★★   Two or three pitches. Either bring two ropes (two raps to ground) or downclimb (6) to the right. Pro: Bolts, longer runners helpful.

353   **Girls (9 R)** ★   Take the left start for this two pitch route. Two ropes (for rappel) recommended. A (9 R) variation start lies to the right. Pro: Bolts, longer runners helpful.

HALL OF HORRORS

This fine area lies about one mile northeast of Ryan Campground, on the west side of the Sheep Pass Road. A series of car pullouts on the right and left sides of Sheep Pass Road (also the parking area for the Saddle Rocks) will be found here. Please follow the climber trail/markers to reduce impact in this area. See the map.

SOUTH HORROR ROCK

The southernmost rock, closest to the road. See photo.

354   **Garden Angel (10a)** ★   Pro: Three bolts.

355   **Lazy Day (7)** ★   Pro: To 2.5 inches.

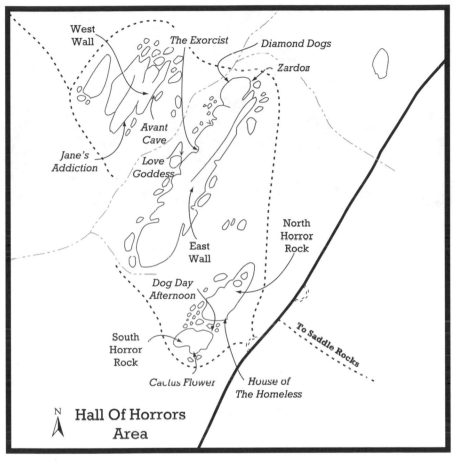

Hall Of Horrors Area

356 **Cactus Flower (11b)** ★★ Pro: Small camming units and bolts/bolt anchor. (The direct start is anywhere from (12a) to near impossible depending on how tall you are.)

357 **Dog Day Afternoon (10b)** ★★ This route lies opposite Grit Roof, on the Southern rock; steep face climbing. Pro: Five bolts, med nuts, two bolt anchor/rap.

NORTH HORROR ROCK

The northern rock, closest to the road.

358 **Houses of The Homeless (8+)** ★ Pro: Three bolts, bolt anchor.

359 **Grit Roof (10c)** ★ Pro: To 4 inches.

HALL OF HORRORS

South Horror Rock
354   Garden Angel (10a) ★
355   Lazy Day (7) ★
356   Cactus Flower (11b) ★★

357   Dog Day Afternoon (10b) ★★
North Horror Rock
358   Houses of The Homeless (8+) ★
359   Grit Roof (10c) ★

HALL OF HORRORS – EAST WALL (West Face)

The main "Hall" lies west of the formation that is next to the road. Most of the established routes lie within the canyon formed by two long domes. See map, page 85.

NORTHEAST END ROUTES

The following routes lie on the northeast end of the main (center) Hall of Horrors formation. These routes share a two-bolt belay, which lies on the slab beneath the summit. Descent: 80 foot rappel from the two-bolt anchor or a Class 3 walk off (toward the top of formation, then around the east side to easier ground near Num's Romp). See map, page 85.

360   **Zardoz (8 R)** ★   Climb straight up face to a small square roof which is passed on the right. Above, continue up face to a two-bolt belay. A few small nuts can be placed under the small roof near bottom. Pro: Thin to 1 inch.

361   **Lickety Splits (7 R)** ★   Start to the right of the previous route and climb the thin crack/flake which leads to unprotected, but easier face climbing to the two-bolt anchor. Pro: Thin to 1.5 inches.

362   **Diamond Dogs (10a)** ★★   Start around and right of the previous climbs at a right-facing and large flake. Lieback up the flake, place some gear, then traverse out left, then up, on face climbing. Two bolts protect face moves above to the two-bolt belay. Pro: To 3 inches, bolts.

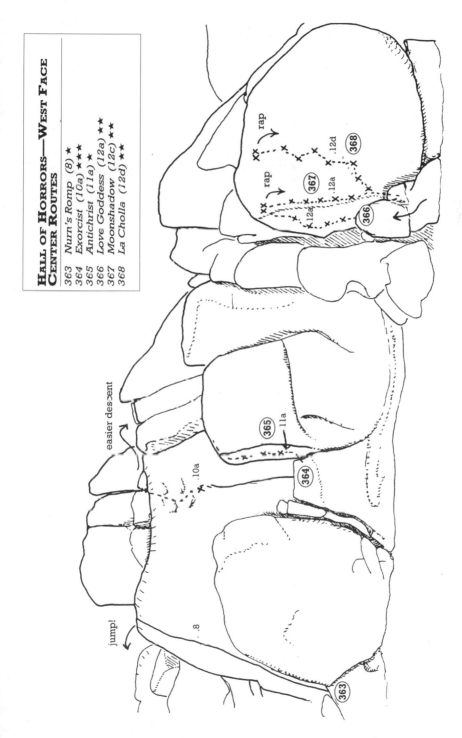

HALL OF HORRORS—WEST FACE
CENTER ROUTES

363 Num's Romp (8) ★
364 Exorcist (10a) ★★★
365 Antichrist (11a) ★
366 Love Goddess (12a) ★★
367 Moonshadow (12c) ★★
368 La Cholla (12d) ★★

WEST FACE CENTER ROUTES

The next several routes are located on the center part of the west face of Hall of Horrors east wall. Many of these end on a interesting summit, meaning the descent is somewhat tricky. The best and quickest (but most intimidating) way off is to walk to the left (northeast) until you must leap across a deep fissure before easier scrambling leads you to the base. More popular is a circuitous and quite grovelly descent to the right. See map, page 85.

363   **Nurn's Romp (8)** ★   Pro: To 3 inches.

364   **Exorcist (10a)** ★★★   Somewhat of a Joshua classic. Pro: Mostly thin nuts, one bolt; take 2 to 3 inches for belay.

365   **Antichrist (11a)** ★   The hardest move is getting off the ground; most jump for the first hold. Pro: Three bolts, 2 to 3 inches for belay.

366   **Love Goddess (12a)** ★★   This is a four-bolt climb on the north side of the large block. Pro: Four bolts.

367   **Moonshadow (12c)** ★★   Climb the northwest arête (to the right of Love Goddess). Easy Class 5 climbing leads to the start, off a small pillar/block. Pro: Seven Bolts.

368   **La Cholla (12d)** ★★   Start as on Moonshadow, but climb up and right. Pro: Eight bolts.

HALL OF HORRORS – WEST WALL (East Face)

A number of fine sport face routes can be found on the West Wall in the Hall of Horrors. Some need nuts for anchors. See map, page 85.

369   **Smashing Pumpkins (12a/b)**   Stick clip first bolt. A very thin and unenjoyable crux at the bottom leads to first bolt. Pro: Three bolts, cams 2 to 2.5 inches.

370   **Jane's Addiction (11b/c)** ★★★   Short people are often stymied by the move past the first bolt. Pro: Four bolts, bolt anchor.

371   **Avant Chain (12a)** ★   A reachy move up high may be the crux for shorter folk. Pro: Four bolts, bolt anchor.

372   **Shaking Hands With The Unemployed (10d R)**   Pro: Two bolts.

373   **Jessica's Crack (6)**   Pro: To 3 inches.

374   **Avant Savant (10d)**   Pro: Thin to medium, one bolt.

375   **Avant Cave (11c)** ★   Pro: Small camming units, bolts, bolt anchor.

376   **Avant Yvonne (11a)** ★   Pro: Three bolts.

377   **Avanti (10d)**   A one bolt wonder.

378   **Read My Lips (11b)** ★   Pro: Small camming units to 2.5 inches; two bolts. Descend right.

HALL OF HORRORS—WEST WALL (EAST FACE)

369 Smashing Pumpkins (12a/b)
370 Jane's Addiction (11b/c) ★★★
371 Avant Chain (12a) ★
372 Shaking Hands With The Unemployed (10d R)
373 Jessica's Crack (6)
374 Avant Savant (10d)
375 Avant Cave (11c) ★
376 Avant Yvonne (11a) ★
377 Avanti (10d)
378 Read My Lips (11b) ★

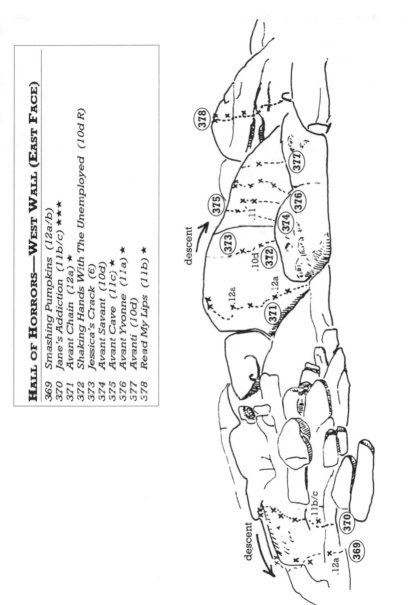

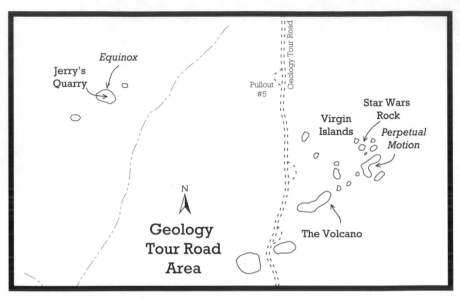

Geology Tour Road Area

GEOLOGY TOUR ROAD

A dirt road heads south from Sheep Pass Loop Road approximately 2.5 miles east of Sheep Pass Campground. This is the Geology Tour Road, so named because of the self-guided geology tour that follows this road. Several climbing areas are located both east and west of this road. The "tour" has several marked stops, numbered sequentially; these marked stops have turnouts that serve as approach parking for climbing areas. Reference to the marked stops is used to assist you in locating approach parking for specific areas.

JERRY'S QUARRY

To approach Jerry's Quarry, park at tour marker #5 (3.7 mile south of Sheep Pass Road). Jerry's Quarry is a complex set of boulders and rocks sitting high off the desert floor about .75 mile west of the road. The northwest side of the formation has an incredible finger crack that goes up and then curves left (Equinox). See map.

> **379   Equinox (12c)** ★★★   The classic first and second knuckle finger crack. Pro: Many thin cams.

VIRGIN ISLANDS AREA

Several piles of rock lie to the east of the parking spot for Jerry's Quarry (about .75 mile south on the Geology Tour Road from Jerry's Quarry parking and 4.5 miles south of the Sheep Pass Loop Road). These are the Virgin Islands. See map.

THE VOLCANO

This large rubble pile/hill lies east of the road. It has a number of very large boulders/rocks scattered along its slopes. The following routes lie near the southeastern end of The Volcano on a large "wave" shaped boulder on the summit of this end of The Volcano formation. This boulder is called the Human Sacrifice Boulder. See map.

HUMAN SACRIFICE BOULDER

380 **Defenders of The Farce (10a)** ★   Climb the northwest face of the Human Sacrifice boulder past one bolt.

381 **Dictators of Anarchy (aka The Skinhead Arete) (12c)** ★★★ This route is located on the south arête of the Human Sacrifice boulder. Pro: Bolts.

382 **New World Order (13b)** ★★★   Just right of Dictators of Anarchy. Pro: Six bolts; chain anchor.

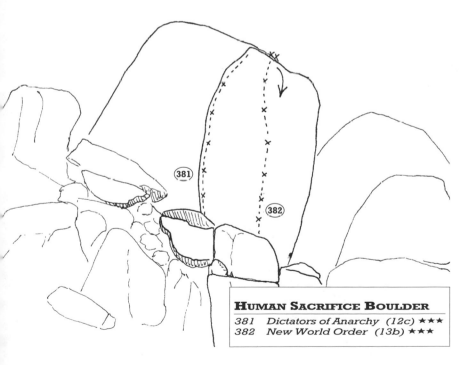

HUMAN SACRIFICE BOULDER
381 *Dictators of Anarchy (12c)* ★★★
382 *New World Order (13b)* ★★★

PERPETUAL MOTION WALL

A conglomeration of rubble piles lies east of The Volcano about 400 yards. A high, level valley rests in the midst of this group. There are two approaches into this valley. This south-facing wall lies on the north side of the high valley mentioned previously. See map, page 90.

383   **Perpetual Motion (10d)** ★★   Near the middle of the Perpetual Motion Wall, climb a vertical thin crack which starts out of a cave-like overhang, just left of a right-diagonalling chimney system. Pro: To 2.5 inches.

STAR WARS ROCK

This rock lies north of the Perpetual Motion Rubble Pile and is easily distinguished by its overhanging south face and the presence of a large split boulder to its south. See map, page 90.

384   **Thumbs Down Left (9)** ★   Pro: To 2.5 inches.

385   **Cedric's Deep Sea Fish Market (10d)** ★★   Pro: Many .75 to 1.5 inches.

386   **Light Sabre (10b)** ★★★   Pro: To 2.5 inches.

387   **Apollo (12c TR)** ★★

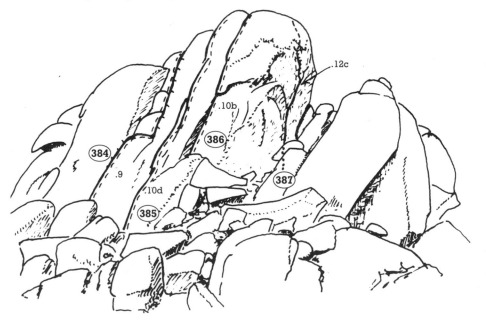

STAR WARS ROCK

384 *Thumbs Down Left (9)* ★	386 *Light Sabre (10b)* ★★★
385 *Cedric's Deep Sea Fish Market (10d)* ★★	387 *Apollo (12c TR)* ★★

SPLIT ROCKS AREA

Take the marked road that heads north off the Sheep Pass Loop Road at a point 1.2 miles past Jumbo Rocks Campground. This road ends at the Split Rocks Parking Lot about 1 mile northwest of Sheep Pass Loop Road.

SPLIT ROCK

Split Rock proper (the large boulder immediately north of the parking area) has been declared off limits to climbing activities by the park. Please respect this closure.

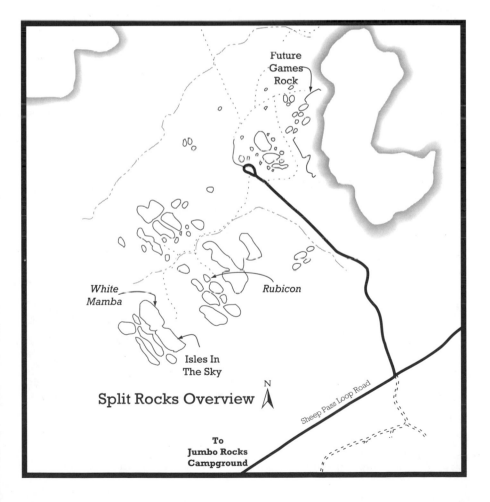

FUTURE GAMES ROCK

This is the steep north-facing face that lies about one mile northeast of the parking lot. See map page 93.

388   **Therapeutic Tyranny (11b/c R)** ★   Hard, weird and scary. Pro: Thin to 4 inches.

389   **The Bendix Claws (11a)** ★★★   An excellent and fun route. Pro: Thin to 1.5 inches, one bolt.

390   **Hang Em High (12b)** ★★   Traditional and funky fun. Pro: Thin to 1.5 inches, three bolts, one fixed pin.

391   **Continuum (8+)** ★★   A good crack pitch. Pro: To 3 inches.

392   **Games Without Frontiers (12c/d)** ★   Crimpy and a little runout. Pro: Thin, three bolts.

393   **Invisibility Lessons (9)** ★★★   A fine, thin and hands crack. Classic for the grade. Pro: To 2.5 inches.

394   **Invisible Touch (10b/c)** ★   Traverse left from Invisibility Lessons to reach discontinuous thin cracks. Pro: Several thin to 2.5 inches.

395   **Disappearing Act (10c)** ★★   Nice face moves, though a little close to Invisibility Lessons. Pro: Thin, four bolts.

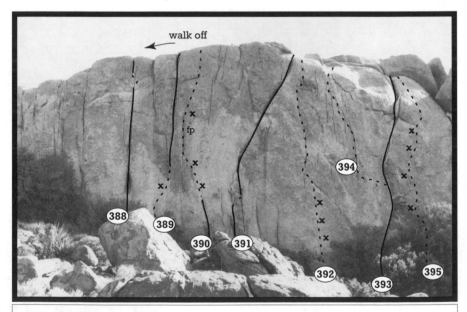

FUTURE GAMES ROCK

388 *Therapeutic Tyranny (11b/c R)* ★	392 *Games Without Frontiers (12c/d)* ★
389 *The Bendix Claws (11a)* ★★★	393 *Invisibility Lessons (9)* ★★★
390 *Hang Em High (12b)* ★★	394 *Invisible Touch (10b/c)* ★
391 *Continuum (8+)* ★★	395 *Disappearing Act (10c)* ★★

SPLIT ROCKS–WEST AREA

The following routes lie to the west of the Split Rocks Parking Lot.

RUBICON FORMATION

This very large boulder/rock is located about .75 miles west of the parking lot.
It faces east. See map. Page xxx. A striking thin crack will be seen on the east
face. This crack (Rubicon) doesn't reach the ground; it starts at a horizontal
crack some 25 feet off the ground. See map page 93.

396   **For Peter (11c R)** ★★   This face climb is found directly across
from the Rubicon Formation (faces west face). Start on the right.
Climb up to and make a scary traverse on a large dike past some
bolts (one may be missing).

397   **Rubicon (10d)** ★★★   This is the crack described above; the
normal start is up a vertical crack on the left, then traverse 25 feet
on a horizontal crack. A direct (unprotected) start up to the crack is
also possible. The direct start is (11+). Pro: Thin to 3 inches.

398   **Seizure (12c)** ★★   Start as on the normal beginning of Rubicon,
but continue straight up the face above the initial hand crack. Pro:
Five bolts (optional to 3 inches).

ISLES IN THE SKY

This formation is about one mile southwest of the Split Rocks Parking Lot.
Several obvious cracks are high on the east face. Easy scrambling leads up
low angled slabs to a ledge system. Descend to the left. Some good cracks
are found in the corridor behind the formation. See map page 93.

399   **Bee Gee (10d)**   This is a four-bolt route on the left.

400   **Nectar (4)**   Pro: Wide stuff.

401   **Dead Bees (9 R)**   Start near Nectar, then head up big holds to
three bolts.

402   **Dolphin (7)** ★   Pro: Bring some big stuff.

403   **Young Guns (11d)** ★   Although this old aid ladder was re-bolted
as a free lead route, it is a little dicey.

404   **Bird of Fire (10a)** ★★   A classic crack up the center of the face.
Pro: Thin to 2.5 inches.

405   **Wings of Steel (11d TR)** ★   Needs to be re-bolted.

406   **Rite of Spring (9)**   Pro: Medium to big gear.

The next two climbs are located on a wall down and to the right of the above climbs. The wall is characterized by large black flakes, a bit of scrambling is necessary to reach the base.

407 **Save The Last Stance For Me (9+)** ★   Start right of a juniper tree, then climb up and right past four bolts to a two-bolt belay/rap shared with the following climb. A little runout.

408 **Slam Dance (10c)** ★   Starts right of the previous climb and climbs straight up, past a bulge and three bolts to the two-bolt anchor/rap shared with the previous climb.

409 **White Mamba (12b)** ★★   Look for a left diagonalling white dike about 100 yards left and below the Isle In The Sky routes. Five bolts lead up and left to a 2 bolt anchor/rap.

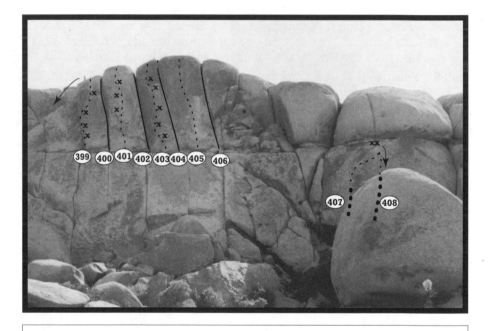

ISLES IN THE SKY

399 *Bee Gee (10d)*	405 *Wings of Steel (11d TR)* ★
400 *Nectar (4)*	406 *Rite of Spring (9)*
401 *Dead Bees (9 R)*	407 *Save The Last Stance For Me*
402 *Dolphin (7)* ★	*(9+)* ★
403 *Young Guns (11d)* ★	408 *Slam Dance (10c)* ★
404 *Bird of Fire (10a)* ★★	

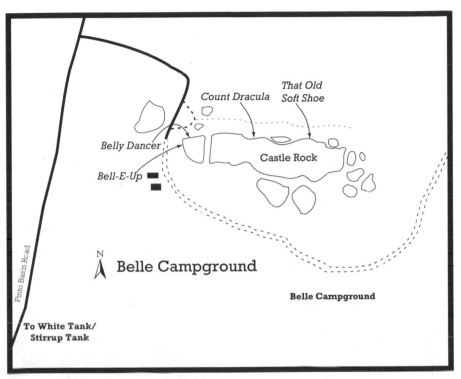

BELLE CAMPGROUND

Belle Campground is located about 1.25 miles south of the Pinto Basin Road from its junction with the Sheep Pass Loop Road. Most of the recorded climbs lie on the large, oblong formation in the middle of the campground, named Castle Rock. Descend down slabs between Diagnostics and Belly Dancer. See map.

CASTLE ROCK – NORTH FACE

410　**Music Box (8)** ★　Pro: To 3 inches.

411　**Bella Lugosi (12a)** ★　The crux is the first ten feet or so, which has gotten more difficult over the years. Pro: A good spotter and thin stuff to 1.5 inches.

412　**That Old Soft Shoe (10d)** ★★　Pro: Six bolts, nuts for anchors.

413　**Bride of Frankenstein (12a TR)** ★　Climb thin face between That Old Soft Shoe and Transylvania Twist.

414　**Transylvania Twist (10d R)** ★　Nasty fall possible getting to third bolt. Pro: 3 bolts, nuts for anchor.

415　**Junction Chimney (2)**

416   **Chimney Sweep** (0)

417   **Count Dracula** (10d) ★★   A stick clip or good spot will help getting to first bolt (which was drilled off an upright picnic table). Pro: Three bolts, nuts for anchor.

418   **Diagnostics** (6) ★★   A excellent route for the grade. Pro: To 2 inches.

419   **Belly Dancer** (10d) ★★   Pro: Three bolts, two-bolt anchor/rap, optional pro for start.

420   **Bell-E-Up** (11c) ★★   This route starts right of Belly Dancer and goes up and left around the corner, passing three bolts, to join Belly Dancer at its last bolt.

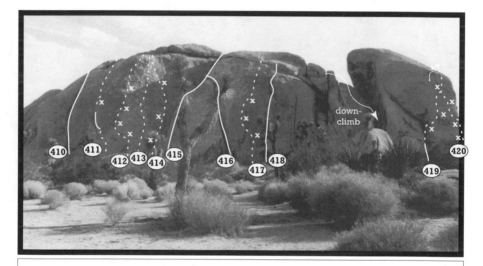

CASTLE ROCK—NORTH FACE

410 Music Box (8) ★	*415 Junction Chimney (2)*
411 Bella Lugosi (12a) ★	*416 Chimney Sweep (0)*
412 That Old Soft Shoe (10d) ★★	*417 Count Dracula (10d) ★★*
413 Bride of Frankenstein	*418 Diagnostics (6) ★★*
* (12a TR) ★*	*419 Belly Dancer (10d) ★★*
414 Transylvania Twist (10d R) ★	*420 Bell-E-Up (11c) ★★*

OZ–EMERALD CITY

Oz is a complex and vast area of rocks that covers an area about 0.5 mile west of Gold Park Road (the road to 29 Palms). This guide only covers selected routes in Emerald City which is best approached from a pullout (interpretive sign located here) on the west side of Gold Park Road about 1.4 miles north of the Sheep Pass Loop Road/Pinto Basin Road intersection. A broad alluvial valley lies to the west. About 1.2 miles up the valley a small *wash/valley opens to your left (south); **Do not** head up this. Walk a little farther and you will see a larger valley/wash heading on your left. It is easily recognized by the large number of huge boulders in the wash. Plan on 35-40 minutes to reach this point from the car. Head up the wash, through the boulders (The Poppie Field Boulders, a number of routes located here), until a flat area above the boulders is reached. A large cliff band will be seen on your left (east).*

THE OZ TOWERS

The following routes are located on a prominent pinnacle set near the far right-hand end of the main band of cliffs.

421 **Sonic Temple (11c)** ★★★ A great sport route on the west face of the pinnacle with five bolts. Two-bolt rap/anchor (toprope anchor for Dave Ate The Cookie).

422 **Dave Ate The Cookie (11d TR)** ★★ Start as for Sonic Temple, but climb up and right.

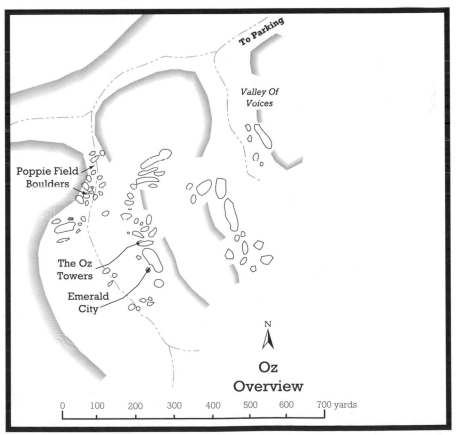

EMERALD CITY

This is the main formation facing west. It has some of the best routes in the entire Oz area.

423 **The Rattler (10d) ★★★**   Pro: To 4 inches, many 1 to 1.5 inches.

424 **Yellow Brick Road (11c) ★★★**   Pro: Eight bolts; two-bolt anchor.

425 **In The Green Room (9)**   Pro: To 4 inches.

426 **Is That A Munchkin In Your Pocket (11b TR) ★★**

427 **Snake Book (11a) ★★★**   The very attractive dihedral on right end of cliff. Pro: Many to 2 inches, two-bolt anchor/rap.

428 **I'm Melting (12a) ★★**   Three bolts protect this route.

INDIAN COVE

This area is located along the northern edge of the Wonderland of Rocks, roughly 1000 feet lower in elevation than other parts of the park. It is located just south of Highway 62 (29 Palms Highway), about nine miles east of the town of Joshua Tree. There, a small sign and some buildings point the way for the remaining three miles to Indian Cove Campground. Aside from being isolated from the other climbing areas of the park, Indian Cove tends to have generally warmer temperatures and is less subject to the high winds that are the bane of winter climbing at Joshua Tree. Because so many climbs start behind campsites, the park's "Occupied Campsite Rule," particularly applies in Indian Cove. This "rule" states that the beginning or ending of a climb in an occupied campsite is only allowed when you have the permission of the person occupying the site.

PIXIE ROCK

This popular rock lies just to your right (west) as you enter the campground. The right-hand edge of the south face is an extremely steep, bucketed face. To the left is a lower-angled slab.

429   **Lascivious Conduct (11c)** ★   Pro: Three bolts, two-bolt anchor/rap.

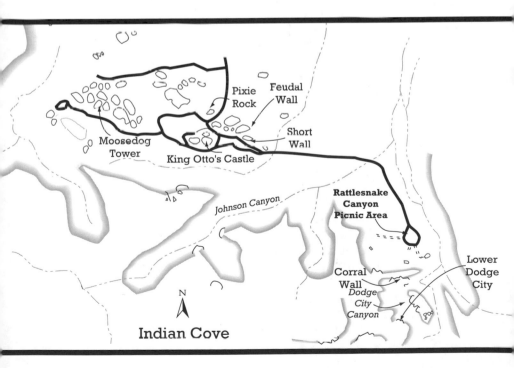

430 **Vaino's Lost In Pot (aka The Scam) (7 R/X)** Unprotected. Either toprope it or you are third classing. Pro: Gear needed for TR anchor.

431 **Who's First (6)** ★ Pro: To 2.5 inches.

432 **Rhythm Of The Heart (8 X)** Pro: None.

433 **Silent Scream (10a)** ★★ Pro: Four bolts, gear to 2.5 inches for anchor.

434 **Silent But Deadly (11b)** ★★ Pro: Three bolts, gear to 2.5 inches for anchor.

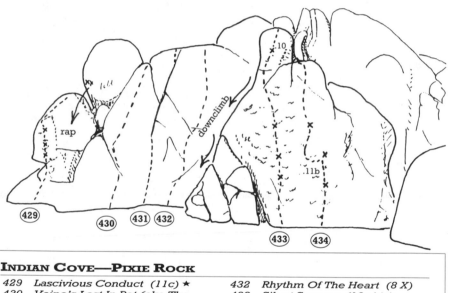

INDIAN COVE—PIXIE ROCK

429 *Lascivious Conduct (11c)* ★	432 *Rhythm Of The Heart (8 X)*
430 *Vaino's Lost In Pot (aka The Scam) (7 R/X)*	433 *Silent Scream (10a)*★★
	434 *Silent But Deadly (11b)* ★★
431 *Who's First (6)* ★	

MOOSEDOG TOWER

This formation liesin the western end of the campground. Rappel off the upper north side. See map, page 101.

435 **Lucky Charms (7)** Start far up the gully (about 100 feet left and uphill from Third Time's A Charm). Climb a corner up and right to intersect Third Time's A Charm. Continue up and right to the ridge to join Tranquility, etc. Pro: To 2 inches.

436 **Third Time's A Charm (10b)** ★★ Two pitches. Crux is face climbing past the bolt where the crack thins out. Pro: Thin to 2 inches, one bolt.

437   **Wandering Winnebago (9 R)** ★   Two or three pitches. Pro: To 2
      inches.

438   **Direct South Face (9)** ★★   A nice line that is easier than it looks. 2
      or 3 pitches. Pro: To 2 inches.

439   **Tranquility (6)** ★   A fun route on the right side of the south
      buttress of the rock. Pro: To 2 inches.

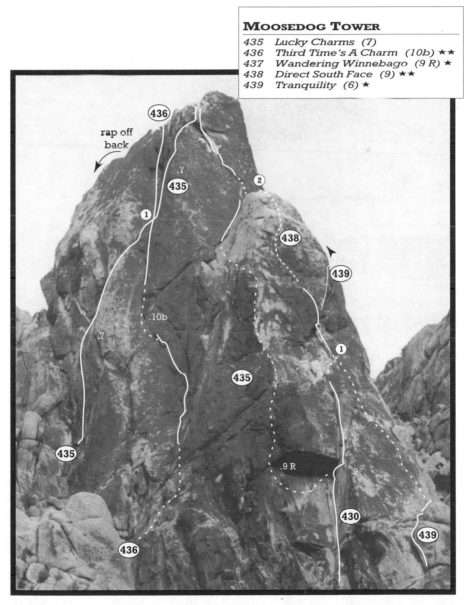

MOOSEDOG TOWER	
435	*Lucky Charms (7)*
436	*Third Time's A Charm (10b)* ★★
437	*Wandering Winnebago (9 R)* ★
438	*Direct South Face (9)* ★★
439	*Tranquility (6)* ★

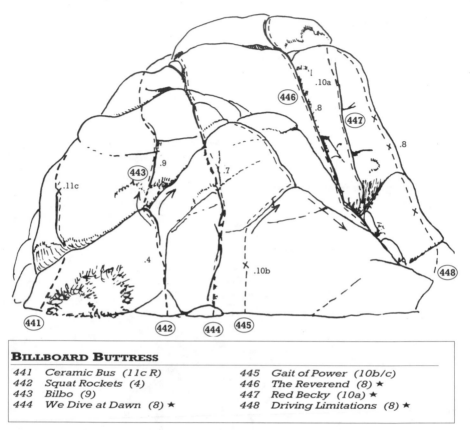

BILLBOARD BUTTRESS

441 *Ceramic Bus (11c R)*	445 *Gait of Power (10b/c)*
442 *Squat Rockets (4)*	446 *The Reverend (8) ★*
443 *Bilbo (9)*	447 *Red Becky (10a) ★*
444 *We Dive at Dawn (8) ★*	448 *Driving Limitations (8) ★*

KING OTTO'S CASTLE

This formation lies on the south side of the crags in the very center of the campground. It is a large squarish block facing south, near the campground road. Several face climbs have been done on this formation. The following route is the right hand of several bolted routes on the main face.

    440   **Sweat Band (10c) ★**   Start right of the center of the face, climb up past a horizontal crack, then more or less straight up past five bolts. Rappel from bolt anchor on the summit.

BILLBOARD BUTTRESS

This small face lies just east of the split in the road as you enter the campground. A parking area and message board make this a stopping point for many climbers. The buttress is about 100 yards south of Pixie Rock, facing west. See map page 101.

    441   **Ceramic Bus (11c R)**   Pro: Thin to 2.5 inches.

    442   **Squat Rockets (4)**   Pro: To 2.5 inches.

443   **Bilbo (9)**   Pro: To 2.5 inches.

444   **We Dive at Dawn (8)**   ★   Pro: Thin to 2 inches.

445   **Gait of Power (10b/c)**   Pro: One bolt, thin to 2 inches.

446   **The Reverend (8)** ★   Pro: To 2.5 inches.

447   **Red Becky (10a)** ★   Pro: Three bolts, nuts for anchor.

448   **Driving Limitations (8)** ★   Pro: Three bolts.

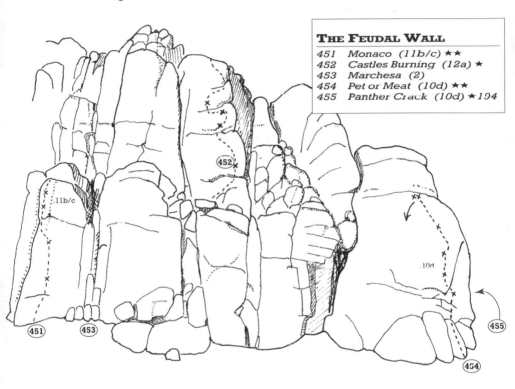

THE FEUDAL WALL

451   *Monaco (11b/c)* ★★
452   *Castles Burning (12a)* ★
453   *Marchesa (2)*
454   *Pet or Meat (10d)* ★★
455   *Panther Crack (10d)* ★194

THE FEUDAL WALL

A large formation lies above a small wash/canyon on the north side of the road and to the right (east) of Billboard Buttress and Willit Pillar. This is the Feudal Wall. The low formation forming the south side of the wash/canyon is the Short Wall. See map page 101.

449   **Pocket Pool (11d)** ★   This five bolt route lies on the south face of the section of rock just left of La Reina on the upper portion of the right-hand part of the Feudal Wall.

450   **La Reina (9)** ★   This route and the previous climb lie on the upper left end of the main Feudal Wall. This route is the very

obvious right-facing corner high on the face. Descend to the left.
Pro: To 2.5 inches.

451   **Monaco (11b/c)** ★★   Pro: Four bolts.

452   **Castles Burning (12a)** ★   Pro: Four bolts, nuts to 2 inches.

453   **Marchesa (2)**   Pro: To 2 inches.

454   **Pet or Meat (10d)** ★★   Pro: Four bolts, two-bolt anchor/rap.

455   **Panther Crack (10d)** ★   The right slanting and overhanging
      crack about 40 feet around the corner and to the right of Pet or
      Meat. Thin to 2.5 inches.

SHORT WALL

*This wall lies just south of the Feudal Wall, facing the main campground road.
All the following routes lie on the right-hand side of the south face. This is a
popular spot for novices and for top-roping activities. See map page 101.*

456   **Left V Crack (11b R)** ★

457   **Right V Crack (10a)** ★★

458   **Face To Face (11c TR)**

459   **Linda's Crack (2)**

460   **Linda's Face (6 R)**

461   **Chockstone Chimney (4th Class)**

462   **Tight Shoes (7 R)**

463   **Double Crack (3)**

464   **Up To Heaven (8 R/X)**

465   **Toe Jam Express (3)**

466   **Steady Breeze (7 X)**

467   **SOB (6)**

468   **Morning Warm-Up (10a X)**

469   **Afternoon Shakedown (11a X)**

470   **Gotcha Bush (4 R/X)**

471   **Right N Up (8 X)**

472   **Donna T's Route (5)**   The crack near the right end of the south
      face.

SHORT WALL

456 Left V Crack (11b R) ★
457 Right V Crack (10a) ★★
458 Face To Face (11c TR)
459 Linda's Crack (2)
460 Linda's Face (6 R)
461 Chockstone Chimney
    (4th Class)
462 Tight Shoes (7 R)
463 Double Crack (3)
464 Up To Heaven (8 R/X)
465 Toe Jam Express (3)
466 Steady Breeze (7 X)
467 SOB (6)
468 Morning Warm-Up
    (10a X)
469 Afternoon Shakedown (11a X)
470 Gotcha Bush (4 R/X)
471 Right N Up (8 X)
472 Donna T's Route (5)

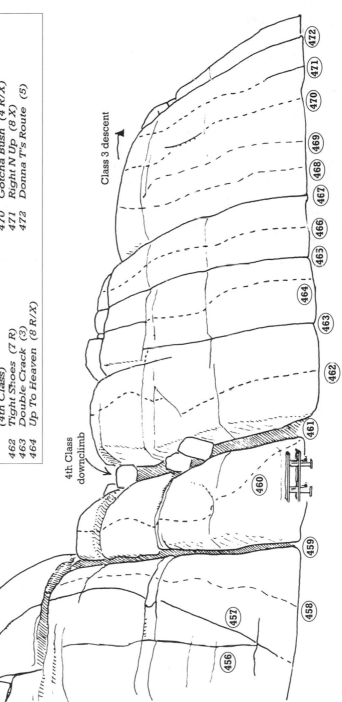

Class 3 descent

4th Class
downclimb

THE CORRAL WALL

This crag faces south. It is one of the warmest crags at Joshua Tree, and has good moderate climbs. It lies in a side canyon off Rattlesnake Canyon, to the southeast of the campground. The approach is quite short (15 minutes). From Indian Cove Campground take the road heading southeast from the vicinity of the Short Wall to where the road ends at a picnic area; park here. From the car, walk a short bit east to the Rattlesnake Canyon wash. Head south (up the canyon) for about 400 yards. At this point, the wash has turned to the southwest (right) and then makes an abrupt turn back east (left). The terrain becomes more jumbled past this point. Where Rattlesnake Canyon turns sharply back east, head straight (southwest) up boulders through an obvious notch. Over the notch, the terrain levels (with lots of bushes and good trails). Immediately to your right (north) is the south-facing Corral Wall. Stay on established trails and leave this area in BETTER shape than you found it. See map page101.

473   **Honky Justice (12a/b)** ★   Pro: Thin cams, fixed pin, two bolts, two bolt anchor/rap.

474   **Only Outlaws Have Guns (9+)**   Pro: Three bolts, cams, two-bolt anchor/rap.

475   **Six-Gun By My Side (10a)** ★   Pro: Five bolts, two-bolt anchor/rap.

476   **Party In The Desert (10b)** ★★   The cliff classic. Pro: To 2 inches, three bolts, two-bolt anchor/rap.

477   **Wild Wild West (11a)**   Pro: Five bolts, two-bolt anchor/rap.

478   **Hang 'Em High (10a)** ★   Pro: To 2 inches, three bolts, two-bolt anchor/rap.

479   **High Noon (10b R)** ★   Pro: To 2 inches, two bolts, two-bolt rap.

480   **Exfoliation Confrontation (10a)** ★★   Four bolts, two-bolt anchor/rap.

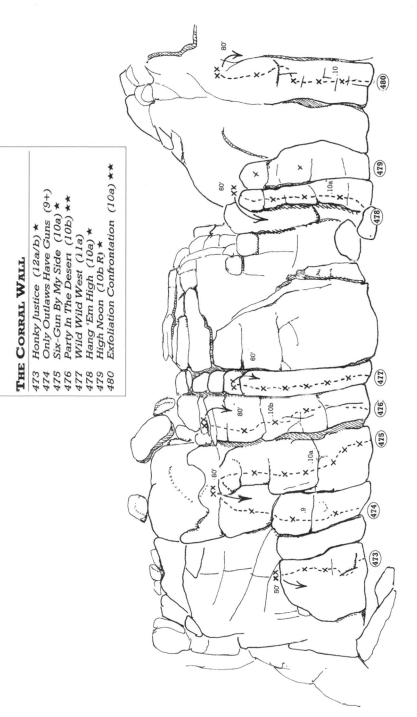

The Corral Wall

473 Honky Justice (12a/b) ★
474 Only Outlaws Have Guns (9+)
475 Six-Gun By My Side (10a) ★
476 Party In The Desert (10b) ★★
477 Wild Wild West (11a)
478 Hang 'Em High (10a) ★
479 High Noon (10b R) ★
480 Exfoliation Confrontation (10a) ★★

INDEX

This is an index of named routes and features only. Formations of areas are in all capitals.

Access: It's everybody's concern

The Access Fund, a national, non-profit climbers' organization, is working to keep you climbing. The Access Fund helps preserve access and protect the environment by providing funds for land acquisitions and climber support facilities, financing scientific studies, publishing educational materials promoting low-impact climbing, and providing start-up money, legal counsel and other resources to local climbers' coalitions.

the **ACCESS FUND**

Climbers can help preserve access by being responsible users of climbing areas. Here are some practical ways to support climbing:

- **Commit yourself to "leaving no trace."** Pick up litter around campgrounds and the crags. Let your actions inspire others.

- **Dispose of human waste properly.** Use toilets whenever possible. If none are available, choose a spot at least 50 meters from any water source. Dig a hole 6 inches (15 cm) deep, and bury your waste in it. *Always pack out toilet paper* in a "Zip-Lock"-type bag.

- **Utilize existing trails**. Avoid cutting switchbacks and trampling vegetation.

- **Use discretion when placing bolts and other "fixed" protection.** Camouflage all anchors with rock-colored paint. Use chains for rappel stations, or leave rock-colored webbing.

- **Respect restrictions that protect natural resources and cultural artifacts.** Appropriate restrictions can include prohibition of climbing around Indian rock art, pioneer inscriptions, and on certain formations during raptor nesting season. Power drills are illegal in wilderness areas. *Never chisel or sculpt holds in rock on public lands, unless it is expressly allowed* – no other practice so seriously threatens our sport.

- **Park in designated areas,** not in undeveloped, vegetated areas. Carpool to the crags!

- **Maintain a low profile.** Other people have the same right to undisturbed enjoyment of natural areas as do you.

- **Respect private property.** Don't trespass in order to climb.

- **Join or form a group to deal with access issues in your area.** Consider clean-ups, trail building or maintenance, or other "goodwill" projects.

- **Join the Access Fund.** To become a member, *simply make a donation (tax-deductible) of any amount.* Only by working together can we preserve the diverse American climbing experience.

The Access Fund.
Preserving America's diverse climbing resources.
The Access Fund • P.O. Box 17010 • Boulder, CO 80308